MORE PET BUGS

A KID'S GUIDE TO CATCHING
AND KEEPING INSECTS
AND OTHER SMALL CREATURES

Sally Kneidel
Illustrated by Mauro Magellan

John Wiley & Sons, Inc.
New York • Chichester • Weinheim • Brisbane • Singapore • Toronto

This book is dedicated to the students and readers
who have written me such enjoyable letters: Laquanda Mosley,
Eunice Peguese, A. J. Glover, Carson McBain,
Merry K. Smith, Nicholas Kwilinski, and others.

The Publisher and the author have made every reasonable effort to ensure that the experiments and activities in this book are safe when conducted as instructed but assume no responsibility for any damage caused or sustained while performing the experiments or activities in the book. Parents, guardians, and/or teachers should supervise young readers who undertake the experiments and activities in this book.

Library of Congress Cataloging-in-Publication Data

Kneidel, Sally Stenhouse.
      More pet bugs : a kid's guide to catching and keeping insects and other small creatures / Sally Kneidel ; illustrated by Mauro Magellan.
         p.   cm
      Includes index.
      Summary: Provides information about the physical characteristics, habitats, and behavior of various insects and tells how to catch and keep them for observation.
      ISBN 0-471-25489-4 (pbk.)
      1. Insects as pets—Juvenile literature. 2. Pets—Juvenile literature.
   [1. Insects as pets. 2. Pets.] I. Magellan, Mauro, ill. II. Title.
   SF459.I5K577   1999
   638—dc21   98-51625

Printed in the United States of America

10 9 8 7 6 5 4 3 2 1

CONTENTS

INTRODUCTION

Insects and other creatures of a similar size are perhaps the easiest animals to study. We see them every day, even in the city. A small amount of observation can lead to surprising discoveries. Consider earwigs, for example. Many people think of earwigs as disgusting pests. But did you know that earwigs are very tender mothers, often guarding and protecting their babies for weeks, until the young are half grown? Mother earwigs are happy to carry out their motherly duties in a terrarium, where you can watch them.

Do you know why whirligig beetles whirl? What beetle has an ugly wormlike larva, with tough jaws, that hides in its burrow and ambushes prey? What insect looks just like a praying mantis but isn't? You'll find out all these things here, and how to keep each of these creatures in your home so that you can really get to know them.

What Are Bugs and What Are Insects?

What is a bug? Technically, a bug is an insect in the order Hemiptera. But the word *bug* is also commonly used to mean any insect, or any very small creeping or crawling creature.

What is an insect? An insect is an animal that has an **exoskeleton** (a hard outer covering), six jointed legs, and three body parts: a head, a **thorax** (center section), and an **abdomen** (rear section). Wings and legs are attached to the thorax.

Many types of insects have two pairs of wings. Sometimes only the second or back pair is used for flight. When this is the case, the first pair are thicker and serve as wing covers, covering and protecting the second pair when the insect is not in flight. Wing covers are called **elytra**. Beetles are one group of insects that have elytra.

Insects have two different kinds of life cycles. One type of insect life cycle is called **complete metamorphosis.** In complete metamorphosis, an egg hatches into a **larva,** which is more or less wormlike. The larva's job is to eat and grow. It sheds its skin periodically as it grows. When it has grown as much as it's going to, it becomes a **pupa.** The pupa is inactive, and does not eat. It is enclosed in a silken cocoon, or perhaps in a tough skin, where it transforms into an adult. This transformation is called a complete metamorphosis. The larva and adult usually do not look at all alike, often live or move around in different places, and often have different diets. In this book, ants, mantis flies, all the beetles, and all the moths undergo complete metamorphosis.

The other type of insect life cycle involves what is called **gradual** or **incomplete metamorphosis.** In gradual metamorphosis, an egg hatches into a nymph, which is not wormlike. It has legs and often looks very much like the adult, but without wings. It often lives in the same habitat as the adult and has the same diet. The nymph eats and grows rapidly, shedding its exoskeleton at intervals. (This is called **molting.**) The last time it sheds, it emerges from the exoskeleton as an adult with wings. In this book, earwigs, grasshoppers, crickets, milkweed bugs, box elder bugs, and dragonflies all undergo gradual metamorphosis.

All insects are **cold-blooded.** This doesn't mean that their body temperature is always low. It just means that their body temperature is not regulated internally like that of humans and other **warm-blooded** animals. Their body temperature is determined by the temperature of the air, water, or surfaces around them. Cold-blooded animals can regulate their body temperature somewhat by sitting in the sun or moving out of the sun.

If a warm-blooded animal's body temperature drops very low, the animal will often die, unless it is hibernating. But a cold-blooded animal can tolerate gradual chilling (not as low as 32°F, 0°C). As its body temperature drops, the animal just slows down. Eventually it slows so much that its muscles stop working. But it is still alive. In the book, I sometimes suggest chilling insects in the refrigerator for a few minutes to slow them down so you can move them from one container to another. This doesn't hurt them; it happens on a regular basis in nature. However, the freezer can kill them, if they're left in it for more than one minute.

Warm-blooded animals eat much more often than cold-blooded animals. Most of the energy we get from our food goes toward maintaining our body temperature. Our body is like a house with a furnace that burns fuel all day long to keep the house warm. Cold-blooded animals get their warmth from their environment, so they don't need to eat nearly as often as we do.

The Noninsect Bugs

The last section in this book introduces you to spiders, snails and slugs, earthworms, planarians, and crayfish, none of which are insects. Spiders are arachnids and can be easily distinguished from insects by their eight legs and two body segments. Snails and slugs are mollusks, soft-bodied animals that have no skeleton. Often they live in a shell. Earthworms are annelids, a group of worms that all have segmented bodies. Planarians are flatworms. They are long and flat, and unlike the annelids, are not segmented. Crayfish are crustaceans, just as crabs and lobsters are. Crustaceans are related to insects and spiders, since they are all in the large phylum Arthropoda.

How This Book Is Organized

Each chapter in this book covers a particular insect or other small creature. The first section of each chapter tells you what the bug looks like. The second section describes where to find it. In the third and fourth sections, you'll find information about catching the bug and keeping it in captivity. The last section of each chapter tells you some interesting aspects of the bug's behavior.

Throughout this book, the common names of particular species are capitalized, such as Large Milkweed Bug, Small Eastern Milkweed Bug, and European Earwig. Common names that apply to more than one species are not capitalized, such as milkweed bug, earwig, and water scavenger beetle.

In the Appendix you'll find an explanation of how insects and the other animals in the book are categorized by scientists. The Appendix also tells where you can order milkweed bugs, fruit flies for feeding the mantis flies and house spiders, insect collecting nets, aquatic nets, and some other items mentioned in the book.

The first time a word from the Glossary is mentioned in the book, the word will be in bold print. Words about the classification of insects are all mentioned in the Appendix, which begins on page 103.

A Few Pointers about Catching and Keeping Insects and Other Small Creatures

1. **When you flip over logs or stones looking for bugs underneath, always return the log or stone to its original position.** It's home to many creatures you may not see. The dampness and crevices underneath are just as they like it. If you don't leave the log or stone as you found it, no creatures will be there the next time you look.

2. **If you put a creature in a jar to take indoors for a day or two, always place a slightly crumpled, damp (not soggy) paper towel in the jar with it.** The paper towel will provide cracks and crevices for your creature to hide in and cling to. It will also provide moisture. Most of the dead insects that children bring to me in jars have died from lack of moisture. Your paper towel will need to be moistened daily with a few drops of water or a spray bottle.

   A plastic quart-size peanut butter jar is a good temporary container because it's transparent and it won't break if you drop it.

3. **Most insects and small creatures will not drink water from a dish.** Never put a dish of water in a container that you're carrying around, because it is very likely to slosh out and drown your pet. Even in a terrarium that isn't being moved, a bug may stumble into a dish of water and drown. In nature, most tiny creatures get their moisture either from dewdrops or through their skin. The best way to water them is by spraying droplets throughout the con-

tainer every day and, in some cases, keeping the soil or sand they live in damp.

4. **To make a suitable lid for a jar, use a piece of cloth as a lid, held in place with a rubber band.** Plenty of air passes through cloth, but tiny creatures cannot escape through it.

    If your pet bug clings to the cloth lid, thump the cloth before removing it. If a cloth lid is not readily available, you can ask your parents to poke holes in metal or plastic jar lids.

5. **Always put a lid on a terrarium, unless a chapter specifically says you don't need to.** Many of the terrarium sizes mentioned in the book correspond roughly to the variety of plastic terraria with plastic snap-on lids that are commonly available in pet stores and pet departments. These terraria are larger at the top than the bottom; the dimensions I give are for the bottom. The lids to these terraria have slots for air. If you don't have a lid, you can make a lid of cloth held in place with a rubber band. Glass terraria sometimes come with a different kind of lid, which is fine as long as air can circulate. Recommended terrarium sizes are approximate.

6. **Aquatic animals do best in the same water you found them in.** You can also use bottled spring water from a grocery store, but don't use distilled water. A third option is to use tap water that has been standing uncovered for 24 to 48 hours. Chlorine will evaporate from water over a period of time. Or you can use drops from an aquarium store to dechlorinate tap water instantly. When replacing water that has evaporated, you can use water right from the tap, as long as the new water doesn't add up to more than one-fourth of the total new volume of the aquarium.

7. **Handle your pet bugs carefully.** Like all animals, insects need to be handled gently and carefully. A pinching grasp, between two fingers, is likely to injure or kill many of these animals. But a grasp between two fingers is appropriate for grasshoppers, because they're hard-bodied, they kick, and they can bite. Pay attention to the instructions in particular chapters for the other animals that can bite or pinch, such as ground beetles, tiger beetles, dragonfly nymphs, and possibly earwigs. These may bite if you close your hand around them. But if you hold your palm completely open and flat, or let them walk on the back of your arm, they probably won't. It's difficult to generalize because there are many species of ground beetles, tiger beetles, and dragonflies. Watch the jaws of your captive while touching its body gently with a twig. Does the creature snap its jaws or try to bite the twig? Use this as a guide for whether and how to hold it.

Whirligig beetles and water scavenger beetles have mouthparts that could bite, although I've never known them to or found any mention of their biting. But again, be cautious. Observe their behavior with their jaws before holding.

Be careful when holding insects not to alarm them. If you do not put a fingertip or fold of skin in front of their jaws, then they will have no reason to bite.

Some people use "bite" and "sting" interchangeably, but here a "bite" is a pinch with the jaws, and a "sting" is the injection of a pain-causing substance. None of the insects in this book sting, except for some species of ants. If you find that ants you are pursuing are biting or stinging you, leave them alone and find some different ones.

Insects You Should Not Pick Up

Velvet ants are almost 1 inch (25 mm) long and look like they're covered with red velvet. The female is not winged and looks very much like an ant, although velvet ants are really wasps. Females give a painful sting. They wander alone over the ground, not in groups like most ants. Of course, you know not to touch the ants' relatives, the bees and wasps.

There are many aquatic insects that are **predators** (animals that kill other animals) and will bite or sting. Diving beetles (in the genus *Dytiscus*) are predatory beetles that live in water. Many species are tiny, but larger species may bite. You can tell whirligig beetles from diving beetles by their whirling behavior. You can tell water scavenger beetles from diving beetles by the clubbed antennae on the water scavengers. Also, the water scavenger beetles come to the surface for air with their heads up, while the diving beetles come to the surface with tail up, head down.

Other aquatic predators to beware of are giant water bugs and back swimmers. Both are hemipterans and have the X pattern on the back, created by the edges of the folded wings, which is characteristic of all hemipterans. Back swimmers swim on their backs. Giant water bugs can be more than an inch long, and look a little like roaches. Both have stinging mouthparts.

Some terrestrial hemipterans that are predators, particularly the assassin bugs, can give painful stings, too, with their tubular mouthparts. In general, you should not hold hemipterans (X pattern on the back) on bare skin unless you know for sure they are plant eaters. Those that eat plants, like the milkweed bug and the box elder bug, are harmless.

Some caterpillars have bristles that sting, particularly the Saddleback Caterpillar, which is green with a brown spot on the back.

Don't pick up any spider unless a grown-up tells you it's okay. Many spiders bite, and two, the Black Widow and the Brown Recluse spider, are dangerous.

This list doesn't cover everything that could bite or sting, only a few of the more common ones. There are a number of useful field guides listed at the back of this book that can help you identify other bugs. If in doubt, don't touch, just watch.

Tick Warning

If you plan to walk through brush and weeds looking for insects, you should find out if you live in an area where there are ticks that carry Lyme disease and/or Rocky Mountain spotted fever. You can find this out by asking your doctor, or by calling the county health department or the county agricultural extension service. If you do live in an area where ticks carry these diseases, you should wear protective clothing (long sleeves and long pants, socks and shoes, and a hat) and apply bug repellent before you go out. Change and launder your clothes when you come in, and check your body for ticks. If you find one, don't touch it. Get an adult to remove it. You have to be sure to get the head and jaws and not to squeeze its body while removing it.

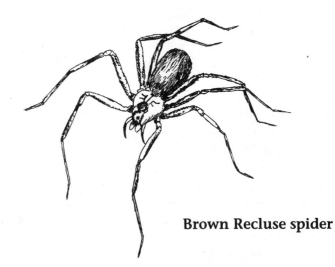

Brown Recluse spider

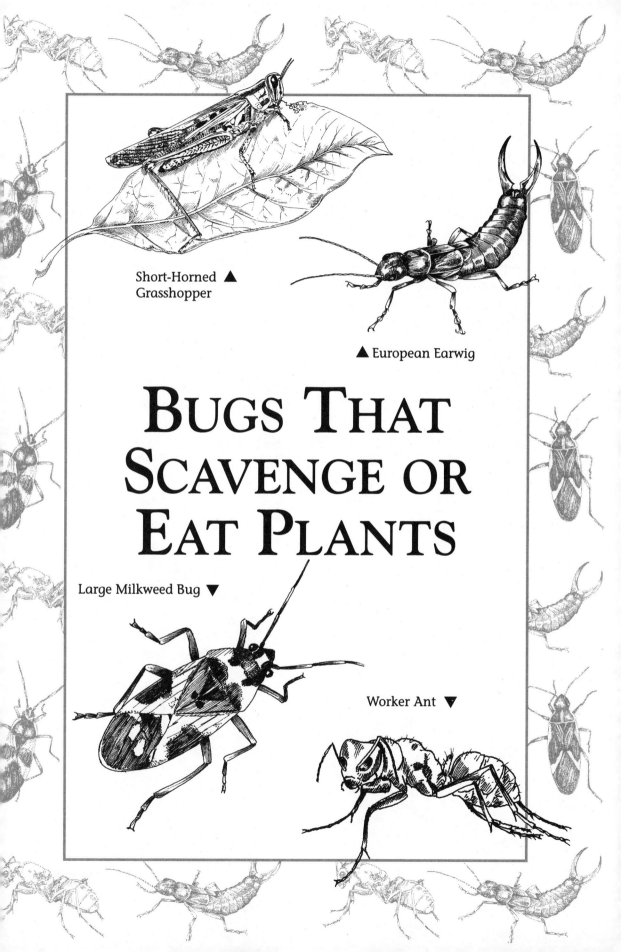

Short-Horned ▲
Grasshopper

▲ European Earwig

BUGS THAT SCAVENGE OR EAT PLANTS

Large Milkweed Bug ▼

Worker Ant ▼

ANTS

What They Look Like

Everyone knows what an ant looks like, but did you know that there are about 10,000 species of ants? On all wingless ants, the three body parts (the head, thorax, and abdomen) are clearly separated and easy to recognize. But the body parts can have somewhat different shapes in different species. Some species are longer or thinner or more long-legged than others. Ants also differ in size and color. Some are less than 1/16 inch (2 mm) long, others as long as 1 inch (24 mm). They can be black, brown, reddish, or yellowish. Black is probably the most common color.

Ants within a single colony can have a different appearance, although they are all the same species. Some may have much bigger heads and jaws than others. The big-headed ones are called **soldiers.** The others are workers, except for the queen, who is often much bigger than the rest.

Ants have distinctive antennae. The antennae are bent as though they have an elbow in the middle. This is not true of ants' relatives, the wasps and bees.

Ants and wasps have a narrow waist between the thorax and the abdomen. The waist of an ant, sometimes called the abdominal stalk, has one or two small humps. Sometimes these humps look like oddly shaped pop beads that join the thorax and abdomen together.

Where to Find Them

Ants are pretty easy to find. Look under logs and near walls, in loose soil. Look for the hills of granular soil that ants have piled up around their holes. Also try looking on plants where aphids live, such as tomatoes, lettuce, and other garden plants.

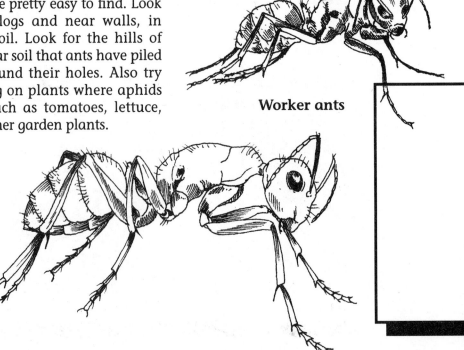

Worker ants

If you don't see any ants around, try putting an apple core in your yard as bait and waiting. It may take a few days (or maybe just a few minutes), but eventually ants will find the core. If not, try another spot. The ants that come to the apple will be worker ants. If the apple doesn't attract ants, try putting a slice of a soft candy bar (like a Milky Way) on the ground near a wall or garbage can. Use sweets that have real sugar in them, not sugar substitutes.

If you locate a line of ants rather than a nest, follow the line back to the nest. You don't need the nest if you want only workers. But if you want the queen you'll need to find where the colony lives.

How to Catch Them

If ants have come to an apple core or other food in your yard, pick up the bait and shake the ants into a jar. Put a lid on it, with no holes in the lid (ants could escape). If you don't want to touch the ants, put the bait in a jar instead of on the ground when you first set out the bait. Lay the jar on its side so the ants can easily get in and out. Then when you go to check on the bait, just pick up the jar with the bait and ants inside. Put the lid on it quickly.

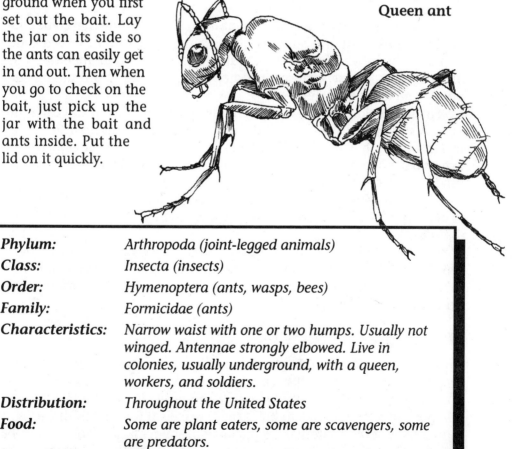

Queen ant

Phylum:	Arthropoda (joint-legged animals)
Class:	Insecta (insects)
Order:	Hymenoptera (ants, wasps, bees)
Family:	Formicidae (ants)
Characteristics:	Narrow waist with one or two humps. Usually not winged. Antennae strongly elbowed. Live in colonies, usually underground, with a queen, workers, and soldiers.
Distribution:	Throughout the United States
Food:	Some are plant eaters, some are scavengers, some are predators.

If you've found a line of ants or a nest of ants without using bait, you can get them into a jar by using a small paintbrush. Hold the jar under the ants or against the ground in front of the ants and brush them in. You'll get sand and plant parts, too, but that's okay.

How do you catch the queen? Occasionally you may get lucky and find the queen inside a rotten log that is easily broken apart. She is generally twice as big as the workers, maybe more. Her abdomen may be quite large, because it's full of eggs.

You can try to get a queen from an underground nest. Dig with a shovel until you reach the nest. Put the entire contents of the nest onto a newspaper. Then use a spoon to pick up what you want to take. Put the small white eggs, the small wiggling larvae, and the larger white pupae or cocoons into a small bag or jar. The eggs are round and no bigger than a worker's head. But the pupae are oval and closer to the size of a worker's body. The queen may be much larger than the workers. Don't forget to take some workers, at least 15, because the queen and her young can't manage without them.

Any disturbance to the nest is likely to bring out soldiers. The soldiers are workers with big heads and big biting jaws. They will bite, so be careful. Some species of ants sting as well as bite. Those that have two beads or humps to the abdominal stalk that joins thorax to abdomen are more likely to sting. Those with one bead or hump belong to a different subfamily and are less likely to sting.

Fire ants belong to the two-hump group. You don't want to catch fire ants. A sting from a fire ant hurts and may cause a small blister. If you live in the southern United States, you may want to call the agricultural extension service in your county and ask if fire ants are in your area and ask how to recognize them.

If you find only workers, that's okay. They alone are entertaining. Try to get about 30 in your jar. They'll take care of themselves and will live for a few weeks.

If you get the workers and a queen, the workers will take care of themselves and the queen, and she will produce more workers and new soldiers. Your captive colony can go on for much longer. Queens sometimes live as long as 15 years!

How to Keep Them

Ants are hardy. They need only food, water, natural sand or soil, fresh air, and a mild temperature. It's best to keep them in clear containers, so that you can see what's going on below ground level. To be able to see them, you have to force the ants to build their tunnels right next to the glass or plastic sides of the container. So the layer of soil next to the glass must be made very thin. You can do this by putting something like a can, a smaller jar, or a block of wood into the center of a glass or plastic jar. Fill the space around the object with *slightly* damp sand or fine soil. This forces the ants to build their tunnels in the space between the outer jar and the inner jar or block. Leave a space of about an inch at the top. A gallon jar is great if you can find one that big. If not, use a quart jar or a large peanut butter jar.

To make a lid, put a piece of cardboard over the mouth of the jar. Mark two spots on the cardboard for holes that will open into the space where the sand or soil is. Get a grown-up to help you make the holes, each about ½ inch (about 1 cm) in diameter. Now put glue all the way around the rim of the jar and put the cardboard in place, with the holes over the sand. Press the cardboard into the glue.

After the glue has dried, get your ants ready to move by chilling them to slow them down. Put the bag or jar you carried them home in into the fridge for a couple of hours, or until none of the ants are crawling around. (Since they aren't warm-blooded, this doesn't hurt them. See the Introduction for an explanation.) Then take the chilled ants and prepared jar outside. Put the ants through one of the holes so that they fall onto the sand in their new home. Plug both holes with cotton when not in use. Air will pass through the cotton. You can also ask an adult to poke tiny holes in the cardboard with a needle if you want to, but it isn't necessary.

When the ants are not near the hole, add some food in very small amounts. The food will get moldy fast on the damp

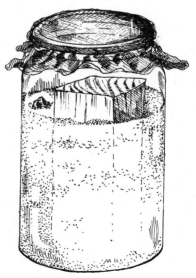

Ant jars

sand, so don't put in more than a pea-size amount at one time. Remove moldy food through the hole with tweezers.

Feel the sand occasionally. If it feels dry, dribble a little water into the second hole with an eyedropper or a small spoon. It must be kept damp, but not sodden. Always put the cotton back in place when you've finished feeding, watering, or cleaning. Be sure, too, that the lid to your ant home stays glued on tightly so that the ants don't get out into your home.

What do you feed ants? Try a few grains of sugar, crumbs of bread or cake or cookie, a tiny shred of cooked meat, a freshly killed small insect, a drop of pancake syrup or honey on a piece of foil, a tiny caterpillar or maggot, or a tiny piece of fruit or vegetable.

What They Act Like

There is something very peculiar about ants and their relatives, the wasps and bees.

Worker ants, although they are all female, do not have their own children. Instead they raise new workers in the colony, children of the queen, as though those eggs, larvae, and pupae were their own.

Ants, wasps, and bees are referred to as social insects because many of them live in large groups. In these groups, all individuals work toward the good of the colony as a whole. How does a new colony begin?

A new colony can begin at only one time during each year. At that time, the queen lays eggs that will develop into adults with wings. Unlike the workers, these adults are fertile. They will be able to have their own offspring. Some are male and some are female. They fly away from the colony and mate with other winged ants from other colonies.

After mating, each winged female has all the sperm she will ever need to produce fertile eggs for many years. The male dies after mating. Each female crawls under a rock or log by herself and rubs her wings off. She is developing into a queen. Her body digests the wing muscles and body fat, and she begins to lay eggs. After a few weeks some of the eggs hatch into larvae. She feeds some of the unhatched eggs to the larvae. The larvae grow and then turn into pupae. Inside each pupal skin a worker ant is forming.

When the workers emerge from the pupal skins or cocoons, they are all white. The first ones are small, since as larvae they didn't get much to eat. Soon they darken and then go out looking for food for the queen. From then on, they devote their lives to caring for the queen and her offspring (their sisters).

One of the workers' jobs is to make the nest bigger. They make several underground rooms, all connected with tunnels. The queen stays in one chamber for her whole life, taken care of by workers. Her body gets much larger. The eggs she produces are carried by workers to another chamber.

When they hatch, the larvae are fed and tended by workers. The pupae also have a chamber to themselves. Workers help them crawl out of their cocoons when they are ready. These new workers replace the old workers as they die.

Some of the larvae from the queen's eggs will develop into soldiers—the workers that have large heads and jaws. A soldier's job is to defend the colony against attack. Colonies may be invaded by predators looking for larvae and pupae to eat. Or they may be invaded by other ants. Some species of ants invade other colonies and carry away the young to serve as slaves inside their own colonies. Some species of ants don't even have their own workers other than soldiers. They rely totally on slave workers from other colonies to tend their queen and young.

Ants can be not only slave keepers but farmers, too! Many ant species have evolved a relationship with aphids that benefits both the aphids and the ants. Aphids suck juices from plants, and with the plant sugars they eat, they produce a sweet fluid called honeydew. An ant can stroke an aphid in a way that signals the aphid to release a drop of honeydew. The ant takes the honeydew into its crop, or storage stomach, and takes it home. The crop is different from the stomach that digests the ant's own food. Back inside the colony, the ant regurgitates the honeydew and feeds it to other workers, the queen, or young.

You may see a line of ants walking one behind the other for a long distance. Why do they walk in a line like that? They are following a chemical trail. The workers that made the trail used chemicals from their abdomens. The ants can smell or taste the chemical with their antennae. In this way an ant who finds a good food source can lead the other workers to it, so they can help bring the food back to the colony. If a trail is disrupted, the ants become confused. You can observe this for yourself. If you find a line of ants, drag your finger or a stick across the trail to create a gap of an inch or so. When the ants reach the gap, they will seem disoriented. They'll search the area until they pick up the trail again, laying down new chemicals over the gap.

EARWIGS

What They Look Like

Earwigs are slender, flattened insects usually about ½ inch (12 mm) long. They are easily recognized by the large pincers at the hind end of their bodies. No other commonly known insects have pincers in that spot on the body. The male's pincers are thinner and more curved than the female's. The pincers on the female are thicker and straighter, only slightly curved toward each other.

Most earwigs have wings. But even so, most species can't fly. Some species don't even have wings. Those that have wings have four. They have two leathery front wings. And they have two flimsy, transparent back wings. This means that the back wings are like plastic wrap, but not as floppy. These **membranous** back wings fold up in pleats like a fan. If the earwig flies, it uses the back wings for flight. The leathery front wings cover up the back wings when they are not in use.

Surprisingly, the most common earwig in the United States is the European Earwig. Our native American species are not seen very often. The European Earwig is believed to have come to this country in a potted plant, on a ship. Its body and pincers are reddish brown. The antennae, legs, and front wings are dull yellow or yellowish brown; the underside is yellowish brown. It's a medium-size earwig, from ½ to ¾ inch (10 to 15 mm) in length. The many species native to the United States are similar, but may vary in color and size.

Where to Find Them

Look for earwigs in dark, damp places, such as under logs, boards, big rocks, or other ground litter. Earwigs are **thigmotaxic**, which means that they are attracted to places where their bodies

Adult male European Earwig

can be in close contact with more than one surface, like crevices and cracks and the spaces under rocks.

How to Catch Them

During the day, earwigs hide in their dark, damp places. Being **nocturnal**, they come out only at night to look for food. They don't sting, but some species can give a pinch with that big pincer if they're upset and you give them a chance to.

Since most don't fly, they are easy to catch. Take a jar with a lid, a spoon, and a flexible piece of thin cardboard with you when you go looking. Look gently through damp leaf litter for earwigs. Flip over logs, boards,

Earwig nymph

and stones. When you finish, put each log, board, and stone back where it was. If not, you'll be ruining someone's home.

Lay the open jar flat on the ground facing the earwig. Then scoop up the little creature with either a spoon or the cardboard and slide it into the jar. It won't stay in the spoon long, so be quick. If you can't scoop it, use the spoon or cardboard to chase it in. Their bodies are easily injured, so be careful not to scrape over the earwig with the cardboard, or crush it against the rim of the jar.

Put a cloth lid on to transport the earwig home and secure the cloth with a rubber band. It can't fly out but it can crawl or run. Some species are faster than others.

How to Keep Them

Earwigs do well in captivity for a long time if you are careful not to let the soil dry out.

Phylum:	Arthropoda (joint-legged animals)
Class:	Insecta (insects)
Order:	Dermaptera (earwigs)
Family:	Several
Characteristics:	Long and flattened bodies. Front wings short and leathery, like a short jacket. One pair of large forcepslike pincers on the hind end.
Distribution:	Throughout the United States
Food:	Plants or dead organic matter

Put at least 1½ inches (4 cm) of damp soil into the bottom of a terrarium that measures 12 by 7 inches (30 × 18 cm) or so. Put a small piece of rotting wood from an old log on top of the soil. Don't use wood that has been treated with chemicals, like lumber from a store. A piece as big around as the lid of a quart jar is big enough. If you can't find a piece of wood, a rock that size will do. I prefer wood just because it's not as heavy, and so I am less likely to crush the earwig if I look under its hiding place later.

I keep a folded piece of a damp paper towel, as big as a saltine cracker, draped over the wood. Earwigs seem to like to get between the wood and the paper towel. If you try this, keep the paper towel moist by wetting it every day.

If the lid to your terrarium has slots in it, put a thin cloth cover over the terrarium before snapping the lid on. Earwigs are excellent climbers and can easily fit through small spaces.

Spray the terrarium every day, or sprinkle water on it. Check the dampness of the soil every day, too. The soil must be kept damp, but not sodden. If it dries out, the earwig will die. If you need to add water, add one spoonful at a time. Soil only an inch or two deep can get soaked with a very small amount of water. Once you've gotten it too wet, it's next to impossible to get the water out without tearing up the whole terrarium.

What to feed an earwig? They eat mainly dead plant matter and parts of living plants. Some of their favorite plant parts are fruits and vegetables. Try half a grape, a piece of apple, or a small piece of potato. Earwigs sometimes eat slow-moving animals, too, such as snails, aphids, and insect larvae. If you find some aphids, you could offer those. I've also given them a sprinkle of dry crumbs from the bottom of a dog food bag. Dog food is made mainly from grain and it's full of nutrients.

Since they come out to eat only when it's dark, I've never actually seen them eating in the cage. But I know that they do eat in captivity. Since the terrarium is damp, any uneaten food will become moldy after a few days. Remove the moldy stuff with a spoon.

What They Act Like

I've had the good fortune to stumble upon a mother earwig with a nest full of children. Since earwigs undergo gradual metamorphosis, the young look very much like the mother and are called nymphs. The mother was about ⅝ inch (16 mm) long, the youngsters were about ³⁄₁₆ inch (5 mm). All were in a small hole of the size you'd make if you poked a finger into the soil halfway up to the first knuckle. The mother hovered around the hole nervously, her pincer raised into the air and open.

I scooped up the whole bunch with a spoon and put them gently into an empty peanut butter jar. The youngsters huddled together in a little clump. I was amazed to see their mother run over to them and cover them with her body, like an arching bridge. I had never seen an insect behave in such a motherly way. I put about an inch of soil into a different jar, put a tennis ball–size piece of wood on the soil, and sprinkled my earwigs gently onto the soil next to the wood. (Always put in the wood or stone before the earwigs so you won't crush them. They can make their own way under it.)

When I picked up the rock three weeks later, I saw that mama earwig had hollowed out a marble-size burrow. The young ones were in the burrow. One raised its opened pincer as if to threaten me. The young had not all grown at the same rate, and some were twice as big as others. They seemed as cozy as a litter of puppies, resting atop one another in the little burrow. The mother was nearby, but not with them.

Could a mother earwig really chase away a predator? She does have a large pincer, which works. If you uncover your earwig suddenly, it will curl its abdomen until its pincer is pointing straight up. Then the earwig will slowly open the two sides of the pincer, so it is ready to pinch.

How likely is an earwig to pinch you? You can hold an earwig safely in the palm of an outstretched hand. There is little to pinch on a flat palm. However, the creature won't stay there long. Earwigs prefer dark, close spaces, so it will be off and running, looking for a dark crevice. When holding one, I would not put a moving fingertip within reach of its pincer.

Earwigs have another means of defense against predators, in addition to the pincer. They can release a substance from their abdomens that smells like tar or creosote. Probably not very tasty.

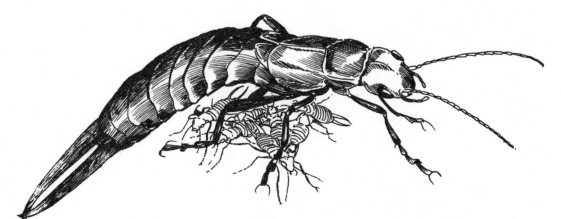

Mother earwig protecting nymphs

GRASSHOPPERS

What They Look Like

The easiest way to recognize a grasshopper is by its long, powerful back legs. They are designed for long jumps. The "knee" of each back leg sticks up way above the body. Grasshoppers also have large heads. Their faces especially are very long from forehead to mouth. They have large compound eyes and chewing mouthparts, but their jaws open sideways rather than up and down like our own.

Most grasshoppers are green or brown to blend in with their surroundings. They have two pairs of wings. The outer pair are long, stiff, leathery strips. They serve just as covers for the second pair, which are used for flying. The wings for flying are membranous—like clear stiff cellophane or plastic wrap. They fold up in pleats like a fan when not in use. Then they can lie neatly hidden by the outer pair. Young grasshoppers, or nymphs, look just like adults except that they have no wings, or very small wings that don't work.

There are hundreds of species of grasshoppers. They range in length from ½ to 6 inches (1 to 15 cm). All have a saddlelike cover (the **pronotum**) over the first part of the thorax, which is just behind the head. The shape of the pronotum can be useful in telling one type of grasshopper from another.

Grasshoppers are closely related to crickets. It's difficult to make a clear rule for telling a cricket from a grasshopper, because there are so many different kinds of each. But in general, crickets do not fly while most grasshoppers do.

The two largest groups of grasshoppers are the short-horned grasshoppers (suborder Caelifera) and the long-horned grasshoppers (suborder Ensifera). The short-horned have antennae that are usually less than half the length of the body, and the long-horned have antennae that are usually as long as or longer than the body.

Most of the grasshoppers you see are probably short-horned. The group of

Short-horned grasshopper

short-horned grasshoppers has many subgroups within it, including the band-winged grasshoppers, which have stripes or colors on their back wings; the slant-face grasshoppers; and the spur-throated grasshoppers. Check out a book called *A Field Guide to the Insects* by Donald Borror and Richard E. White for pictures of all these plus more descriptions.

Where to Find Them

A good place to look for grasshoppers is along paths, trails, and quiet roadsides, or in fields where grass and weeds have become overgrown.

How to Catch Them

You may be able to catch a grasshopper with a jar in cool weather, because cold slows them down, but the best tool to use is an insect-collecting net, sometimes called a "sweep net." A sweep net, made for sweeping through weeds, has a long handle and a cone-shaped mesh net at least 2 feet (60 cm) long. It's not the same as a butterfly net. An insect net or sweep net is sturdier. You can order one from a biological supply house. (See the Appendix for addresses.) Or you may be able to find one at a local science museum shop or science hobby shop.

Sweep the net quickly back and forth as you walk through the weeds. It does no good to sweep the same spot more than once. Most insects you miss will either drop to the ground, or hop or fly away.

Many of the insects that you sweep into the net will fly out unless you close the net when you are not in the act of sweeping. Do this by turning the handle a half turn, which also turns the metal ring that supports the net. The net will then be folded over at the top, draped over one side of the ring.

To empty an insect net, knock all the insects to the bottom of the net by sweeping the net around, open, at top speed. The force of the swinging will keep them from flying out. Then grasp the net with your hand about

Phylum:	*Arthropoda (joint-legged animals)*
Class:	*Insecta (insects)*
Order:	*Orthoptera (grasshoppers and crickets)*
Family:	*Several*
Characteristics:	*Large, flat-sided heads. Strong, thick back legs for jumping. Two pairs of wings. Chewing mouthparts. Usually brown or green.*
Distribution:	*Throughout the United States*
Food:	*Plants*

8 inches (20 cm) above the bottom, or just above where you can see the insects collected. Be careful that you don't grab a bee or wasp. (If you hear buzzing that sounds like a bee, let the bee out, even if your other bugs get out, too.)

You're going to turn the lower part of the net inside out into a plastic quart jar. Many of your insects will escape the first few times you do it, but with practice it gets easier. Not everyone does it the same way. What I do first is turn the upper part of the net inside out, all the way down to where my fist is holding it closed. Then I put the jar against the pinched opening, remove my hand, and push the bottom part of the net down into the jar, turning it inside out as it goes. As quickly as I can, I put the lid over the jar and slowly pull the net through the gap around the lid until the net is all the way out. I snap the lid closed and I'm done.

If you have a grasshopper in the jar, chill the entire jar in the refrigerator until all the bugs are still. This doesn't hurt them because they're not warm-blooded animals.

Grasshoppers do not sting. But they do have strong jaws for chewing plants, and some will bite you if you hold them so that they can. Pick them up by putting a single finger on either side as you would if lifting a sticky candy bar.

How to Keep Them

Use a terrarium at least 12 by 7 inches (30 × 18 cm) for a grasshopper 1 inch (25 mm) long or longer. If you want the grasshopper to lay eggs, you will need to put 3 to 5 inches (7 to 13 cm) of soil in the bottom of the terrarium. If not, a bare floor will do.

Your little friend will want branches or stems to climb on. Pick some leafy branches from the area where you found the grasshopper. Stick one or two into the soil so that they stand upright, at least partly. You can add some extra household food that the grasshopper might like. On a small flat plate put some washed leafy vegetables such as lettuce, spinach, cabbage, or celery. Try other vegetables, too—maybe tomato and cucumber.

What They Act Like

Grasshoppers normally don't move around too much. One that hatches from an egg in your yard will probably grow up in your yard, lay its eggs in your yard, and die in your yard, too. And usually grasshoppers don't live in groups, but prefer to be alone most of the time.

However, some species of short-horned grasshoppers can undergo a very strange change if they get too crowded and their food plants are all eaten up. These crowded grasshoppers can, over a couple of generations, give rise to grasshoppers that *like* company, that seek out other grasshoppers. This new generation of grasshoppers not only seek out company, but they like to travel. And they do travel, in huge **swarms** (large groups). Why? They are looking for new food. As they go, they eat all the plants they come across. The bodies of the new generation are changed, too, to make them better fliers. They have longer wings, they are slimmer, they have more body fat (for energy), and less water (for less weight).

Grasshoppers that undergo this kind of change are called "locusts." Swarms of locusts can do a tremendous amount of damage to farm crops. In many places in the world throughout history, people have starved because locusts have eaten all their crops.

Grasshoppers have a number of ways to protect themselves from predators. Most of them stay hidden and most are camouflaged. If they *are* found, they can always jump or fly, and many will bite. One type of short-horned grasshopper has an extra trick for avoiding predators. These tricky ones are band-winged grasshoppers, with colors or stripes on their wings. The colors only show when the insect flies. So if a grasshopper takes off in flight, the sudden flash of color can startle a predator. Then they just as suddenly close their wings in mid-flight, once again blending in with the background, and drop straight down into the weeds and become hidden again. It's very hard to tell just where they drop.

Male grasshoppers, like crickets, make noises to attract mates. Short-horned grasshoppers make their noise by rubbing a series of small knobs on the back legs over a scraper on the wing. Long-horned grasshoppers rub a series of ridges on one wing across a scraper on the other wing. Listening for the location of the sound can be a good way to find grasshoppers to catch. You might also enjoy listening for differences in calls. Different types of grasshoppers make different sounds. Crickets make a more musical sound than grasshoppers. If the noise seems to have a pitch or tone to it, so that you can hum a similar pitch, then what you're hearing is probably a cricket's song. If the noise sounds more mechanical, more a scraping sound or a buzz, then it's probably a grasshopper's call.

A sweep net

CAMEL CRICKETS ___ OR CAVE CRICKETS

What They Look Like

Camel crickets are big spidery-looking crickets that you might see in bathtubs or bathroom closets or in sheds or under houses. They like dark, damp places, which gives them the name cave cricket. Their other common name, camel cricket, comes from the high, humped back.

You can recognize camel crickets by their long, hairy legs and their pale, humped backs. Don't they sound handsome? No, they really aren't very pretty. How can you tell the homely camel crickets from their more attractive cousins, the field crickets? Field crickets have straight wings covering their backs. Their wings make a pleasant chirping sound when rubbed together. (Field crickets are described in my earlier book *Pet Bugs*, John Wiley & Sons, 1994.) But camel crickets have no wings, so their backs look segmented and humped. Since they have no wings, they can't chirp. They can't hear either. What's more, their eyesight is very poor. But camel crickets are very well adapted to their dark habitat.

For one thing, camel crickets have very, very long antennae—sometimes more than two body lengths! They use the long antennae to feel around themselves very carefully. In addition to long antennae, camel crickets have very long legs. The legs are so long they may stick up more than twice as high as the humped back. These long legs look like they're covered with hairy stubble. But the stubs are really bristles. Their legs are so long that many people mistake these crickets for spiders.

Camel crickets are light brown with black splotches and *big*. A mature camel cricket can be 2 inches (5 cm) long. Their legs are striped, very much like the legs of the American House Spider.

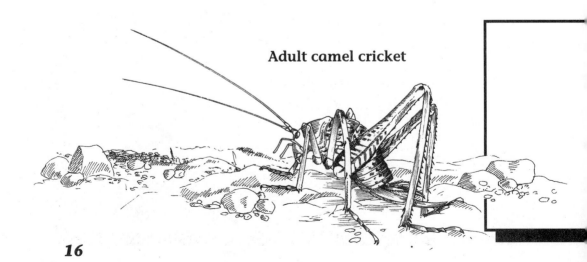

Adult camel cricket

Where to Find Them

Camel crickets and field crickets both like damp, dark places. Field crickets are most often found outdoors—in a leaf pile, a compost pile, a pile of grass clippings, under a piece of plywood, under a garbage bag. But I usually find camel crickets inside structures like a dark shed, a crawl space, or a basement. The place where I find the most camel crickets is in the hole in my yard where the water meter is. If you don't have any of these dark, damp places, ask a neighbor who does.

How to Catch Them

What good does it do a camel cricket to have such long legs? Try to catch one with your bare hands and you'll find out. Camel crickets are good jumpers. Not only do they jump high and fast, but they change directions constantly. So it's hard to predict where they'll be next. But they're still much easier to catch than field crickets. They don't jump as far as field crickets, they don't burrow under things and disappear like field crickets, and they are very clumsy.

Try putting a jar over the cricket. If it jumps away, keep trying, you'll get it eventually. Then slide a piece of cardboard under the jar, and you've got it. If you grab one with your bare hand, the cricket is likely to lose a leg. The back jumping legs break off easily if pulled or pressed. This helps the cricket escape from predators that might grab a leg.

If you can't get one with a jar, try throwing a T-shirt over the cricket, or even a sheet if that doesn't work. You can then slip a jar and a lid under the shirt or sheet and nudge the cricket into the jar from there.

How to Keep Them

Use a terrarium at least 12 by 7 inches (30 × 18 cm). Since camel crickets are attracted to damp and dark places, you need to provide dampness

Phylum:	*Arthropoda (joint-legged animals)*
Class:	*Insecta (insects)*
Order:	*Orthoptera (grasshoppers and crickets)*
Family:	*Gryllacrididae (camel crickets and kin)*
Genus:	Ceuthophilus
Characteristics:	*Humped, wingless backs. Gray or tan. Very long back legs. Long threadlike antennae.*
Distribution:	*Primarily the eastern United States*
Food:	*Dead insects, plants, fungi*

and darkness in the terrarium. Put at least an inch of damp soil or sand on the floor of the terrarium. Over this you might want to put a layer of old decaying grass clippings and leaves. A paper towel roll will make a dark hiding place for the crickets. Or you can make them a little home inside the terrarium by cutting a door in a small cardboard box or milk carton.

Male and female camel crickets in their terrarium

A fresh slice of potato or fruit daily will help provide water. You can also spray the terrarium every day with a plant mister. Sprinkle a spoonful of water over the soil every day or two as needed to keep the sand or soil damp.

Camel crickets are scavengers, which means that they eat dead matter. You can offer them a piece of dried dog food that has been soaked in water to soften it. Or sprinkle in a few crumbs of dried dog food from the bottom of the dog food bag. Try different types of fruits or vegetables or plain bread in very small pieces. Don't offer greasy or salted food.

What They Act Like

All crickets have two feelers at the hind end called cerci. All adult female crickets have a long spine between the two cerci. The spine is an egg depositor, or **ovipositor.** It looks like a long, slim claw on a female camel cricket, at least ½ inch (12 mm) long and curving slightly upward. When she's ready to lay eggs, she will poke it into the ground and the eggs will come out the end of it, one at a time. Since the males and the young have no ovipositor, it's easy to identify the adult females. Crickets undergo gradual metamorphosis, so the young are called nymphs.

Your crickets will explore the terrarium by tapping the walls and floor with their incredibly long antennae. If you have more than one cricket, you will see them communicate by tapping each other's antennae, or by draping an antenna across another cricket. They also communicate with kicks. If a female gets unwanted attention from a male, she will kick him with her muscular back leg and send him flying.

Camel crickets will also use two long, jointed mouthparts to tap-tap-tap the ground as they walk along. These tappers look like bendable drinking straws, but the tappers are bent in two places instead of one. They are called **maxillary palps,** or just **palps.** Every few steps a cricket will pause to eat some tiny speck it has found with its palps.

Camel crickets frequently clean their legs, especially the front ones. It's fun to watch. The cricket moves its mouth carefully down the length of each leg, like a cat. It skips the very top part that it can't reach. If the cricket comes across a piece of something edible, it will pause in its cleaning to chew it up. Camel crickets are not picky eaters!

MILKWEED BUGS

What They Look Like

Milkweed bugs are either black-and-orange or black-and-red bugs that live on milkweed plants. They're about ½ inch (12 mm) long and look somewhat like beetles. You can tell they're not beetles by the way their wings meet on the back. The outer wings of a beetle meet in a line down the middle of the back, and they don't overlap. Milkweed bugs are in the order Hemiptera, the order of true bugs. The wings of all hemipterans cross on the back, so there is no line down the middle. Instead, the edges of the wings make diagonal lines that cross in the middle of the back. Sometimes this makes a clear X on the back on hemipterans, on others just the upper triangle of the X is clearly visible.

One type of milkweed bug is called the Large Milkweed Bug. The way its wings are folded makes a triangle on the back. It has a black underside, black legs, black antennae, and is black at both ends. On its back are two wide red or orange bands, with a black band between them. The head is black with orange markings, and the thorax has orange edges. The nymph is red with black antennae and legs. The nymphs have no wings.

Phylum:
Arthropoda
(joint-legged animals)
Class:
Insecta (insects)
Order:
Hemiptera (true bugs)
Family:
Lygaeidae (seed bugs)
Genus and species:
Lygaeus kalmii (Small Eastern Milkweed Bug), Oncopeltus fasciatus (Large Milkweed Bug)
Characteristics:
Oval body. Black with red markings.
Distribution:
Small species throughout the United States, large species east of the Rocky Mountains
Food:
Milkweed seeds

Large Milkweed Bug

There's another type of milkweed bug called the Small Eastern Milkweed Bug that's about ⁴/₁₀ inch (9 to 10 mm) long, a little bit smaller than the Large Milkweed Bug. Its basic colors are similar but the pattern is a little different. This one also has a black head, with red markings. It has a black underside, black antennae, and black legs. But on the folded wings, on the back, is a red X-shaped mark. The Small Eastern Milkweed Bug has other red markings across its back just behind the head, in front of the wings. These red markings behind the head seem to form a band, although they are really just large spots of color.

Where to Find Them

Milkweed bugs live on the many species of milkweed plants. Milkweed plants are common weeds that usually have milky sap. The leaves on the stem are opposite each other, like the crossbar on the letter **t**. Look for milkweed bugs on the underside of leaves and among the flowers.

How to Catch Them

When milkweed bugs are disturbed, they often let go and drop to the ground. This can work to your advantage when trying to catch them. Just put your container under them before you disturb them, and they'll drop right in. A plastic peanut butter jar works well for catching them. Once your jar is in place, nudge the bug you want with a small paintbrush. If you want several, you may have to work quickly to minimize escapes from the jar. Use the paintbrush to push them back in, or whack the side of the jar. Put the lid on as soon as you can.

Small Eastern Milkweed Bug

How to Keep Them

You can keep two or three milkweed bugs in a terrarium as small as 10 by 6 inches (25 × 15 cm). If you have more and they're crawling over each other and trying to eat in the same spots, try a bigger terrarium. If your terrarium lid has slots in it, put a cloth cover over the terrarium before snapping on the lid.

Put some slightly damp soil in the bottom of the terrarium. They don't really need soil, but slick plastic is not easy for them to walk around on. They might like a couple of twigs to crawl on. A milkweed twig will work, or any dry multibranched twig with the leaves plucked off.

In nature, the females lay eggs on the underside of milkweed leaves. If you want this to happen in your terrarium, you'll need to keep fresh milkweed leaves, still attached to the twigs, inside the terrarium. Putting the cut end of the twig in a small cup of water will keep it fresh longer. You can put a cloth around the base of the twig and cup to keep the bugs out of the water, where they could drown.

If there are no milkweed leaves, the female may lay her eggs somewhere else. You can put stretched-out cotton balls in the bottom of the terrarium instead of soil, so that the cotton covers the bottom. Your milkweed bug may put her eggs on the cotton.

Feed your milkweed bugs seed pods from milkweed plants. If you can't find any of these seeds, the bugs can live for several days with no food. But give them moisture by spraying the terrarium daily with a plant mister, or by keeping a moist piece of paper towel in the terrarium at all times.

What They Act Like

Milkweed bugs are one of the few insects that **migrate** (travel seasonally from one habitat to another). Monarch butterflies are another well-known example. They spend the summer in the United States and Canada, but fly south to Mexico before winter. Cold-blooded animals like insects can't move around at subfreezing temperatures. And there's nothing to eat during a harsh winter. So why don't all insects migrate? Migrating is just one way to get around the problem of freezing winters. Most insects adopt a different strategy for surviving winter. They lay their eggs in fall and then die, leaving only the eggs to make it through the cold until spring. Eggs don't need to move or eat, so it's much easier for an egg to survive winter than an adult insect.

Not all milkweed bugs fly south before winter. Many live year-round in places that are warm enough for overwintering. But even in very cold places, not all of them migrate. Some stay behind and freeze to death.

Milkweed bugs mate and lay eggs in late summer. When exactly depends upon whether they migrate. Those that don't migrate will mate earlier. The others will mate after they migrate.

The eggs will lie dormant over the winter and hatch in the spring. The newly hatched nymphs feed on milkweed seeds and molt into the next generation of adults during the summer.

Milkweed bugs have something else in common with Monarch butterflies. Both milkweed bugs and the caterpillars of Monarchs eat milkweed plants. These plants have poisonous chemicals in them that would kill most insects. But Monarchs and milkweed bugs are immune to them—the poisons don't hurt them. The poisons build up in their bodies, though, and their bodies become toxic to any predator that tries to eat them.

Both milkweed bugs and Monarchs have bright red or orange coloring. Red or orange on any small animal is usually a warning color. Predators know or learn that an insect or animal with warning colors either does not taste good, or will cause illness.

Teachers often buy milkweed bugs when a class is studying insect life cycles. They are a good example of an insect that undergoes gradual metamorphosis, and they will go through the whole life cycle in captivity. You can order them from Carolina Biological Supply Company. (See the Appendix for the address.)

**Milkweed plant
in bloom**

Box Elder Bugs

What They Look Like

Box elder bugs look a lot like milkweed bugs. Both are true bugs, meaning that they belong to the order Hemiptera. The inner edges of the box elder bug's wings form a sort of X across its back, as is true for most hemipterans. This sets them apart from beetles, whose wing covers meet in a straight line down the middle of the back.

Box elder bugs are oval-shaped, somewhat slimmer than milkweed bugs, and about ½ inch (10 to 15 mm) long. They are a dull black, and marked with red along each side. On top of the middle to lower back there is also a fine red line that makes a V pointing toward the head. (This is the bottom half of the X mentioned above.) They also have a short red line down the head-to-tail midline of the body, just behind the head. It looks like the bug has a necktie on backward, on its back rather than its chest. The under surface is red and black.

Box elder bugs are very active, usually walking at a fast pace, seldom resting. They can fly, but don't very often.

Phylum:
Arthropoda
(joint-legged animals)

Class:
Insecta (insects)

Order:
Hemiptera (true bugs)

Family:
Rhopalidae (scentless plant bugs)

Genus: Leptocoris

Characteristics:
Oval-shaped. Black body with edge of front wings outlined in red and an upside-down red V on the back.

Distribution:
Eastern Box Elder Bug east of the Rocky Mountains, Western Box Elder Bug west of the Rocky Mountains

Food:
Box elder trees, other maple trees, and fruit trees

Adult box elder bug

Where to Find Them

Box elder bugs are often seen around box elder trees, which is a type of maple, or around other trees in the maple family.

Although they can be found on these trees at any time other than winter (they suck sap from the leaves), most of the box elder bugs I've found have not actually been on trees, but rather on surfaces of structures *near* box elder trees or other maple trees.

Box elder trees are often planted in parks and on city property, especially in the Midwest. They are popular plantings because they tolerate harsh weather, especially drought, better than many other trees. Late fall and early spring are the best time to look for swarms of box elder bugs.

How to Catch Them

Box elder bugs are quite easy to catch, since they don't bite or sting. They can fly, but I've never seen one fly to avoid being caught. Just sweep them into a jar with your fingers, or a cloth, or a small paintbrush.

How to Keep Them

A good place to keep three or four box elder bugs is a small plastic terrarium—10 by 6 inches (25 cm × 15 cm). You can put some soil and bark on the floor of the terrarium, but the bugs will probably stay on the plastic sides or on the lid all the time, so the soil is unnecessary. Also include a loosely crumpled damp paper towel for the bugs to drink from. Remoisten it every day.

If you have a plastic lid that has slots in it, put a piece of cloth over the opening of the terrarium before clamping the lid on. Otherwise the bugs can crawl through the slots. You can drizzle water through the cloth onto the paper towel inside. This is much faster and easier than taking the lid off to water them. When you do take the lid off, you'll have to be very careful that the bugs don't all escape before you can get it back on.

Box elder bugs overwinter as adults, laying their eggs in the spring. This is unusual; most other kinds of adult insects die in summer or fall, leaving their eggs or pupae to endure the winter and carry on in the spring. Since adult box elder bugs live through winter, they apparently can go long periods without leaves or buds to suck sap from. Box elder bugs

Box elder bug nymph

often spend winters inside human homes, where there is no food or water. So if you catch your bug in autumn, you can probably keep it healthy for months with a damp paper towel for moisture, and no food.

If you catch one in the spring, it will need to eat again fairly soon. If it is uninterested in box elder or maple twigs, you can probably still keep it healthy for a week or two with just moisture. Then you should probably let it go.

As always, keep the terrarium out of direct sunlight.

What They Act Like

Like all hemipterans, box elder bugs have a long strawlike mouthpart for sucking. You may see them sucking up moisture from a paper towel. The tubular mouthpart is hollow and can actually puncture plant tissue, allowing the bug to get to the sap inside the plant.

In spring, the mother bug lays eggs on box elder trees. The hatchlings are red. Like all hemipterans, box elder bugs undergo gradual metamorphosis. So the young red box elder bugs are called nymphs. The nymphs suck sap from box elder trees just like their moms and dads do. So when they hatch, they're in exactly the right place already.

Some hemipterans, such as the stinkbug you may have heard of, give off bad smells. The box elder bug gives off a pleasant smell instead. I have heard it described as smelling like roses, although I haven't smelled it myself.

Box elder bugs seem to have an urge to walk upward, since they always escape within two seconds after I take the lid off of their terrarium. It makes sense that an animal that feeds on tree leaves and doesn't fly much would have an urge to walk up. To test this idea, I put three box elder bugs into an empty paper towel tube and set it vertically, on end, on a tabletop. I covered the top of the tube with black construction paper, anchored with a small book. (I did this to block out light, so that if they did walk up, I'd know they weren't attracted to light from the top.) I checked them every hour or so all afternoon. Two of them were usually at the top. If I turned the tube around, so the bottom was now at the top, they turned around and walked to the top again. The third one was sometimes at the top and sometimes not.

Box elder leaf and seed

All of the box elder bugs that I've accidentally dropped on the floor have walked up the nearest table leg or sofa leg. This is further evidence that they do have an urge to climb. But to get a definite answer about box elder bugs and the urge to climb, I'd need to repeat the paper towel tube experiment with about 10 more bugs. Maybe you'd like to give this experiment a try.

**Box elder bugs
climbing table**

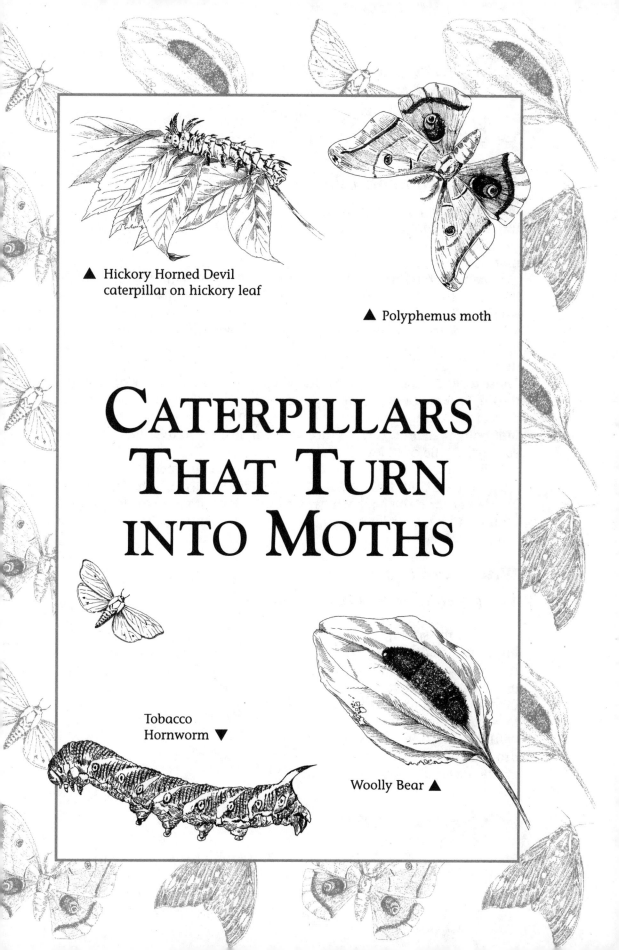

▲ Hickory Horned Devil
caterpillar on hickory leaf

▲ Polyphemus moth

CATERPILLARS THAT TURN INTO MOTHS

Tobacco
Hornworm ▼

Woolly Bear ▲

WOOLLY BEARS
OR WOOLLY WORMS

What They Look Like

A caterpillar is the young form, or larva, of a butterfly or moth. After eating and growing, a larva undergoes complete metamorphosis and becomes an adult. (See the Introduction for more about complete metamorphosis.)

The most famous caterpillar in the United States may be the Woolly Bear. It is the larva of the Isabella Tiger Moth. A Woolly Bear may look woolly, but the densely packed hairs that cover its body are really stiff. If you've ever seen a bottlebrush, you get the idea. This bristly caterpillar is about 1½ inches (4 cm) in length when fully grown. The hairs that cover its body are each about ¼ inch (7 mm) long, and come in two colors. Those on each end of the body are black. Those in the middle are reddish brown, and may have some black ones mixed in. The long hairs or bristles can discourage some animals that might want to eat the Woolly Bear. But many predators, such as raccoons, can just brush the hairs off before eating the little creature.

The adult form of the Woolly Bear, the Isabella Tiger Moth, is a yellowish brown moth with about a 2-inch (5-cm) wingspan. The front wings are darker than the back wings. All four wings are more or less unpatterned and evenly colored, with only a very few tiny grayish or brownish spots on each wing.

Where to Find Them

Most people find Woolly Bear caterpillars crossing roads or paths in the fall or spring. In the spring the caterpillars have just emerged from hibernation and are moving about actively searching for food. In the fall the larva is looking for a place to overwinter safely. It moves around constantly, at a pretty fast pace for a caterpillar.

Woolly Bear

How to Catch Them

Woolly Bears may feel tickly when you touch or hold them, but they are completely harmless. If you find one, just pick it up and put it in a jar. It will continue to crawl, so make sure it can't crawl out, by covering the jar with a piece of cloth, held in place with a rubber band. Air can pass freely through the cloth. If you found it eating a plant, take along some leaves of the plant. Keep the jar out of direct sunlight.

How to Keep Them

The Woolly Bear will need a terrarium at least 12 by 7 inches (30 × 18 cm). Put an inch or two of dampish soil on the bottom of the terrarium. Spray the terrarium every day with a little water, or flick a few droplets of water around the terrarium with your fingers. Keep the soil slightly damp—not wet, but not completely dry.

Feed the Woolly Bear plantain leaves. Plantain grows commonly, and is abundant on lawns. The plant is not difficult to recognize. The leaves are oval-shaped and come right out of the ground, like grass. The main veins in the leaves are *parallel,* which distinguishes this weed from look-alikes. If your parents have your lawn treated to kill weeds, you won't find plantain there. Look in a neighbor's yard. Woolly Bears will eat dandelion leaves, too, although plantain is preferred. (See drawing on page 28.)

If you find a Woolly Bear in the fall, it may be ready to hibernate. Offer it food even though it may have finished eating. It may grab the chance for a last meal before the big winter fast. If you want the Woolly Bear to hibernate in the terrarium, put some flattened dead leaves on the soil and then a large flattish piece of bark. The Woolly Bear may crawl under the leaves and bark if it's ready to hibernate.

Phylum:	*Arthropoda (joint-legged animals)*
Class:	*Insecta (insects)*
Order:	*Lepidoptera (butterflies and moths)*
Family:	*Arctiidae (tiger moths)*
Genus and species:	Isia isabella *(Isabella Tiger Moth)*
Characteristics:	*Very hairy caterpillar, black on both ends and rust-colored in the middle.*
Distribution:	*Throughout the United States*
Food:	*Plantain, dandelion leaves, other low-growing wild herbaceous plants*

If you find a Woolly Bear crawling around in spring, it may have just come out of its winter hibernation. It will probably be quite hungry.

Isabella Tiger Moth

By early to midsummer, after eating for a few weeks, Woolly Bears are ready to **pupate** (change from larvae to adults) and become moths. When they are ready to pupate, they won't eat at all. So if you find a caterpillar in early to midsummer that won't eat, the creature may be getting ready to pupate. Or you may have given it the wrong food.

To make its cocoon, a Woolly Bear will seek out a crevice or the space under a stone or piece of bark. If you have a Woolly Bear in early or midsummer, when it might pupate, you could add to the terrarium some small blocks of scrap wood and bark, stacked in an irregular way to create a wide variety of spaces. Of course, once the animal has made its cocoon, you'll need to leave the wood alone until the moth comes out.

When the moth first emerges, the wings will be crumpled. But they will straighten out and harden as blood is pumped into them. Until the wings have hardened, the moth can't fly and is easy prey for mice or birds.

The best time to let it go is just after the wings are ready, around the time it begins trying to fly. If you let it flutter against the sides of the cage, it will damage its wings. The safest time is dusk or after dark; the safest place is under a bush where it will be sheltered from birds. If you can't wait until dusk or dark, at least put it under a bush or other shelter.

The moth will mate and if it is female, will lay eggs. The eggs hatch into tiny Woolly Bear caterpillars that grow into big Woolly Bear caterpillars by autumn.

What They Act Like

Woolly Bears are faster than most caterpillars. They can walk at a rate of 4 feet (1.2 m) per minute. That's $\frac{1}{20}$ mile per hour ($\frac{1}{14}$ kph)!

Woolly Bears are one of the few moth species that spend the winter in caterpillar form. Most moth caterpillars pupate in the fall, and overwinter inside the hard skin or silken cocoon of the pupa. A pupa is camouflaged and protected somewhat by its thick covering. A caterpillar is more vulnerable to predators and freezing temperatures, so it has to find a safe place to hide for the winter, often under leaves or bark on the ground. When a Woolly Bear finds a protected spot, it curls up into a tight ball and stays that way for the winter. The curled-up position causes the hairs or bristles to poke out in every direction. Eating a rolled-up Woolly Bear would be like swallowing a spiky ball—not too attractive for most predators.

A Woolly Bear will roll into a ball if you pick it up, too, or any time it is disturbed. This lightweight bristly little ball is surprisingly hard to hold on to. It bounces and slips out of your hand like a piece of wet ice.

According to local folklore, Woolly Bears can predict winter weather. It is said that the relative amount of red and black on a Woolly Bear in the autumn will foretell the harshness of the winter to come. Interpretation of the colors varies, but some say that the 13 bands of bristles on the Woolly Bear represent the 13 weeks of winter. Black bristles in a band indicate relatively cold weather for that week.

Woolly Bears are so popular in the mountains of North Carolina, my home state, that the town of Banner Elk has held a Woolly Worm Festival every year since 1978. The festival includes crafts, foods, rides, and the featured event: the Woolly Worm Race. Anyone having a Woolly Bear caterpillar can participate. Each caterpillar must race up a string 3 feet (91.5 cm) long. The grand winning caterpillar gets to be the official predictor of the coming winter.

Woolly Bear caterpillar walking up a string

POLYPHEMUS CATERPILLARS

What They Look Like

The Polyphemus caterpillar is the larva of the Polyphemus moth, a giant silkworm moth. The giant silkworm moths are a group of related species in the family Saturniidae. The moths in this family are the biggest moths in North America. Some have a wingspan of almost 6 inches (15 cm). Although moths in general tend to be a dull brown or gray, most of the giant silkworm moths are more brightly colored. Some have big spots on the wings that look like eyes.

The Polyphemus moth is probably the most common of the giant silkworm moths in North America. It's a big one, with a wingspan of 3½ to 5½ inches (9 to 14 cm). It's also one of our most beautiful moths. As all moths do, it has four wings—two in front and two in back. The wings are brownish yellow. The two front wings each have a pinkish line parallel to the body, about ½ inch (1 cm) away from the body. Near the outer edge of each wing is a black line edged with white, parallel to the outer edge of the wing. Each of the four wings has a distinct eyespot near the center. An eyespot looks like an eye, but it can't see anything. It's just a pattern of colors on the wing. The eyespots on the front wing are yellow and black and round. Those on the back wings are clear in the center, edged in yellow, and surrounded by a bigger oval of dark blue fading into black.

Why do Polyphemus moths have eyespots? From a distance, the eyespots look like the eyes of a bigger animal. The larger eyespots on the back wings are often hidden by the front wings. If the moth is disturbed, it can suddenly uncover the rear eyespots. This sudden appearance of a big pair of "eyes" can startle a bird or other animal that might be thinking of eating the moth.

Polyphemus caterpillar

The body of the adult moth is heavier and thicker than the body of a butterfly with the same size wings. The top part of the body is covered with gold to reddish brown "fur." It isn't real fur because moths are not mammals, and only mammals have true hair or fur. But it looks like fur. Polyphemus moths, and many other giant silkworm moths, have very wide, feathery antennae.

Polyphemus cocoon

The Polyphemus caterpillar is a light, bright green, almost a fluorescent green. The color is surprisingly bright. When fully grown, the charming moth-to-be is about 3½ inches (9 cm) long. It is more plump than most caterpillars. It feels soft to the touch, not prickly at all.

Its body has a series of soft ridges along the back, like an accordion. From each ridge, a thin yellow stripe runs vertically down each side of the caterpillar. Each yellow stripe has along its length four small spots. Along the top of the caterpillar, from head to hind end, is a single row of red bumps with hairlike bristles sprouting from them. The caterpillars of Luna moths look very similar but have a yellowish horizontal line along each side.

Polyphemus caterpillars are slow and sluggish. In spite of their bristles on top, they are completely harmless.

Phylum:	*Arthropoda (joint-legged animals)*
Class:	*Insecta (insects)*
Order:	*Lepidoptera (butterflies and moths)*
Family:	*Saturniidae (giant silkworm moths)*
Genus and species:	Antheraea polyphemus
Characteristics:	*Green caterpillar, accordion-shaped with short, spiky bristles and red spots on each segment*
Distribution:	*East of the Rocky Mountains from Canada to Mexico, more common in the South*
Food:	*Caterpillars feed on oak, hickory, elm, maple, birch, and other trees and shrubs*

All caterpillars have three pairs of legs, just behind the head. These legs are "true legs" because they develop in the same way that other insects' legs develop. They will become the legs of the adult moth, after metamorphosis. The true legs of Polyphemus caterpillars are rather like six small thorns, curving inward. They're not as sharp as thorns, and they won't pierce your skin. But they do feel prickly when the caterpillar grabs a finger.

Having three pairs of legs near the head works fine for an adult moth. But it makes the long caterpillar like a bus with no rear wheels. So the caterpillar has several pairs of temporary legs at the hind end of its body, called **prolegs**. They look very different from the true legs. The Polyphemus caterpillar has five pairs of prolegs. Prolegs are more fleshy than true legs, but they're strong. Prolegs are often used for clinging to a branch while the caterpillar moves its head around to eat leaves. They are also used in walking, of course.

Where to Find Them

Since a caterpillar's job is to eat and grow, it spends almost its whole life on the leaves of its food plant. Many caterpillars will eat only one type of plant. But the Polyphemus caterpillar is not as picky as some. It prefers the leaves of an oak tree, but it will also eat the leaves of hickory, elm, maple, willow, alder, basswood, chestnut, poplar, and sycamore trees.

The caterpillars are much easier to spot on the ground than on leaves. They may even be on a sidewalk, where they're especially easy to see. Late summer is the best time to look for them. If you look too late, they may already be in their cocoons.

The cocoon is roughly egg-shaped or oval. Its color is whitish, although it may be almost entirely wrapped in leaves that are stuck to it. It is more or less the size of a 10-year-old's big toe. The size can vary depending on if and how leaves are attached to it. Polyphemus cocoons are sometimes attached to the end of branches. More often they fall from the branches and lie hidden among the leaves on the forest floor.

How to Catch Them

A Polyphemus caterpillar is quite easy to catch, once you've found one. Just pick it up. If you don't want to touch it, nudge it into a jar. It will be much happier on the ride home if the jar has a cloth or a tightly wedged stick for the caterpillar to cling to. Don't put in a stick that can move around, or a rock, or sand or soil. Loose things in the jar can injure the caterpillar. Cover the jar with a cloth held in place with a rubber band. Don't let the sun shine directly on the jar.

How to Keep Them

You will need a terrarium 12 by 7 inches (30 × 18 cm) or larger for an active caterpillar (one that is not trying to make a cocoon). If your caterpillar isn't already making a cocoon, offer it fresh leaves of oak. If there is no oak, offer hickory, maple, alder, willow, chestnut, birch, elm, basswood, or poplar. Keep the leaves on the stem. The caterpillar cannot get its mouth around a leaf that is lying flat on a terrarium floor. Caterpillars munch the edges of leaves. Put in fresh leaves twice a day, every day. Spray the terrarium every day with a little water, or sprinkle a few water droplets around the sides and bottom with your fingers.

Polyphemus moth

If you find a Polyphemus caterpillar crawling along the ground in late summer and it's 3 inches (7 cm) long or more, then it's probably ready to pupate (make its cocoon). In this case, what it needs is a place to pupate. The caterpillar normally makes its cocoon by wrapping leaves around itself and securing them with silk from its own body. If there are no leaves, it will wrap itself just in silk, attaching the silk to whatever it's resting on.

Once the caterpillar is ready to pupate, it will start making a cocoon whether you are ready or not. So use a terrarium that you don't mind turning over to the caterpillar for the winter—or permanently, since left-over silk may never come off the terrarium. If you want to protect your terrarium from silk attachments, surround the caterpillar with leaves.

What They Act Like

The main activity of Polyphemus caterpillars is eating, which can be interesting to watch. The caterpillar faces the edge of the leaf so that the edge is parallel to its body. It then attaches its jaws to the top of the edge and moves its head down along the edge. In this way, it trims the margin of the leaf. When the caterpillar gets as low as it can go, it detaches its jaws, stretches up, and starts over. As it trims the same edge several times, it creates a C-shaped gap in one side of the leaf.

The biggest reward in keeping a Polyphemus caterpillar is watching it make its cocoon. The caterpillar has no objection to your watching, but you must keep a close eye on it so that you don't miss the show. The whole process takes several hours. The caterpillar begins by attaching a few silk lines to objects around itself. Ideally these objects will be leaves, but if there are no leaves, then it will attach the silk to whatever is there. The silk appears to come from the caterpillar's mouth, but if you look closely you will see that the silk actually comes out of a little tube in the lower area of its face. The tube is less than $1/16$ inch (about 1mm) long. Just above the tube are a pair of structures that look like a pair of piano keys with rounded corners. After the silk comes out of the tube, it goes between the two structures, like dental floss between your two front teeth. The caterpillar seems to guide the silk line with these structures.

Once you see that your caterpillar is making silk lines, you can help it by arranging a number of *fresh* leaves around it. Or place the caterpillar in the center of a large maple leaf, with more leaves around it. The many lobes of a maple leaf are easy for your creature to grab and pull.

As the caterpillar proceeds, it will appear to be just tapping around with its head and true legs and upper body. But as it taps, silk lines will appear on the leaves. At times the caterpillar will grasp and pull a leaf or the lobe of a leaf toward itself while tapping. Over time, the leaves will take on a bowl shape around the caterpillar.

As it works, your little pet will sometimes perform some odd gymnastics to reach a leaf it needs, twisting and turning and doing backbends. You may notice that its body is growing shorter and thicker all the time.

Presently it will pull the leaves entirely around itself. Gaps between the leaves will be filled with silk threads. After the caterpillar has finished, it will release a liquid from its body that will soak into the threads and harden them, to protect the little creature from the coming winter and from some predators. The silken part will then look completely white. Over the next few days, the leaves will dry and wrinkle and the silk will turn light brown, so that the cocoon is barely visible.

HICKORY HORNED DEVILS

What They Look Like

Last year a friend called me and said she had a huge green caterpillar with a bunch of big horns on its head. She said it was the biggest caterpillar she had ever seen, as long as her hand. I knew right away what it had to be. The Hickory Horned Devil is the biggest of the big caterpillars. When fully grown, it can be up to 7 inches (17 cm) long!

The horns are remarkable. Other caterpillars may have bristles and spines, but nothing else has horns like these. Four long horns, not on the head, but behind the head, are swept back as though the beast were facing into the wind. And there are four shorter horns beside them, all of them a flashy orange and black. The horns are covered with sharp spikes that make the creature look quite dangerous, although it isn't. The rest of the long body is adorned with black spikes, six or more per segment.

Phylum:
Arthropoda
(joint-legged animals)
Class:
Insecta (insects)
Order:
Lepidoptera (butterflies and moths)
Family:
Saturniidae (giant silkworm moths)
Genus and species:
Citheronia regalis
Characteristics:
Enormous frightful-looking caterpillar, green with several long, curved orange-and-black horns near the head, smaller black horns along the body
Distribution:
Eastern United States, more common in the South
Food:
Leaves of hickory, walnut, butternut, ash, sumac, sweet gum, and persimmon

Hickory Horned Devil caterpillar on hickory leaf

Older and larger Hickory Horned Devils are mostly green, but the very young ones are black. As they grow, black gives way to brown, which becomes tan, and then finally green.

Royal Walnut moth

Like all caterpillars, the Hickory Horned Devil has six true legs in front—one pair on each of the first three body segments, behind the head. These true legs will reform to become the legs of the moth during metamorphosis. The caterpillar also has five pairs of prolegs toward the rear of the body. The prolegs will disappear during metamorphosis.

Where to Find Them

Hickory Horned Devils are out and about in late summer. The caterpillars spend their young lives in walnut, hickory, sweet gum, pecan, and persimmon trees. They are well camouflaged and unlikely to be seen while feeding. But in September, when they are fully grown, they come down from the trees to find a place to burrow. This is when you are most likely to find them, wandering across the ground.

Try putting up a picture of one in your classroom and ask friends and classmates to be on the look-out for you. If you're going to ask for help, the Hickory Horned Devil is a good creature to choose because it is so easy to recognize.

How to Catch Them

Hickory Horned Devils do like hickory leaves, and they do have horns, but they are not really devilish. All the spikes and horns and spines are just for show. The caterpillars are harmless and easy to pick up.

If you hold one of these caterpillars in your hand, the true legs may grab your finger as though it were a branch. The legs feel pointy and prickly, but are not painful.

You can put it in a jar to take it home. No lid is needed. If there is a hickory tree nearby, or another of its food trees, take some leaves.

How to Keep Them

If you see a Hickory Horned Devil crawling on the ground in late summer, it is probably ready to burrow into the ground and become a pupa. It is probably not interested in eating anymore, or it would be up in the tree where the leaves are. A Hickory Horned Devil may be ready to pupate even if it is only 3 or 4 inches (8 to 10 cm) long.

To get a home ready for one of these caterpillars, put 5 or 6 inches (13 to 15 cm) of soil into a terrarium at least 12 by 7 inches (30 × 18 cm). Since the caterpillar may have just fallen from a tree and may not be ready to pupate, put a few freshly cut stems of hickory, walnut, pecan, sweet gum, or persimmon on top of the soil. The leaves should still be on small branches so that they won't lie flat on the soil. If your caterpillar is eating, change the leaves twice a day every day. Sprinkle a few water droplets over the leaves every day or every other day.

What They Act Like

Your caterpillar will probably start crawling around as soon as you put it in the terrarium. At times it may rear up, lifting its head and six front legs off the ground, as though trying to find something. If it continues to crawl restlessly and does not eat, this is a sign that it may be ready to pupate.

If your caterpillar is ready to become a pupa, you may get to see it burrow underground, or you may just find a hole in the ground where it burrowed when you weren't looking. After it is several inches underground, the caterpillar's body will lose water and shrink to a length of about 2 inches (5 cm). Then the skin at the back of its head will split and the caterpillar will wiggle out of its skin. It will have a new skin underneath that turns brown, but no legs or horns. It's now a pupa, and it will spend the winter underground. When the summer comes, the skin will split again and an adult moth will crawl out.

The adult is not called a Hickory Horned Devil, but has a name that fits its beauty—the Royal Walnut Moth. The name must have been inspired by the beautiful reddish fuzz on its body. The adults are big moths. The female's wingspan may be 5 to 6 inches (13 to 15 cm). The front wings have a gray background color, and a few yellow patches and veins that are highlighted with orange or rust. Overall, the front wings look red-and-gray striped. The back wings are rust-colored with light yellow patches. The body is reddish with yellow markings.

If you are lucky enough to have caught a caterpillar that has gone through this complete metamorphosis, let it go as soon as it has become a moth. The adult has no mouthparts, so it cannot eat or drink. It lives only long enough to find a mate, and if it is a female, to lay eggs. To help a male find her, the female gives off a powerful scent. A male's feathery antennae can detect the smell up to 2 miles (3.2 km) away.

TOMATO AND
TOBACCO HORNWORMS

What They Look Like

Hornworms are huge green caterpillars, though they're not quite as big as Hickory Horned Devils, and not spiny. And they're not quite as brightly colored as the Polyphemus caterpillars. But like the other two, hornworms are big enough to startle anyone. A fully grown hornworm ranges from 3 to 5 inches (7 to 12 cm), and is as big around as a man's finger. Both the Tomato Hornworm and the Tobacco Hornworm are usually green, either light green or dark green, but some may be brown. They are smooth-skinned and hairless. The one thing that tells you a caterpillar is a horn-worm is the single curved horn on top of the hind end of the body. It looks like a sharp stinger sticking up, but it is harmless. The horn of the Tomato Hornworm is black or black and green. The horn of the Tobacco Hornworm is red.

The markings of these two types of hornworms are similar, but not exactly the same. The Tobacco Hornworm has seven diagonal white lines along each side. Each line is above one of the **spiracles**, or breathing holes. The Tomato Hornworm differs in having a white V-shaped mark around each spiracle. (Hornworms and most other insects breathe through spiracles in the abdomen. There is one spiracle for each abdominal segment.)

**Tomato Hornworm with
wasp cocoons on its hind end**

40

The moths that these caterpillars become are also very similar. Both have grayish to brownish wings streaked with beige, black, and brown. Their wings are strong and much narrower than the wings of most moths, and the back wings are pointed rather than rounded. These moths are in a group called the hawkmoths. The adult form of the Tomato Hornworm is called the Five-spotted Hawkmoth. It has five yellow spots along each side of the abdomen (or five pairs of spots along the top of the abdomen). The adult form of the Tobacco Hornworm is the Carolina Hawkmoth. It has six pairs of yellow spots on each side of the abdomen. Both types of moth have a wingspan of about 3½ to 4½ inches (90 to 115 mm).

Where to Find Them

Hornworms are the easiest to find of the three big green caterpillars in this book. That's because hornworms feed on the leaves of common garden plants rather than on the leaves of tall trees as the other two caterpillars do. I have often found hornworms of all ages on the tomato plants in my own garden. They can also eat the leaves of other plants in the tomato family. With a little detective work, you can often tell if hornworms are on your garden plants, even before you see them. Look for leaves with missing pieces. Just one or two hornworms can do major damage to a garden

Phylum:	*Arthropoda (joint-legged animals)*
Class:	*Insecta (insects)*
Order:	*Lepidoptera (butterflies and moths)*
Family:	*Sphingidae (hawkmoths or sphinx moths)*
Genus and species:	Manduca quinquemaculata *(Tomato Hornworm)*, Manduca sexta *(Tobacco Hornworm)*
Characteristics:	*Large green caterpillar with a spot and a white streak or white V on each segment. A single horn pointing backward at its end.*
Distribution:	*Throughout the United States*
Food:	*Caterpillars feed on the leaves of tomato, potato, tobacco, petunia, and other plants in the tomato family.*

plant. Look also for a scattering of green pellets under the plants. These are the droppings of the caterpillar. If you find some, look on a leafy branch above the pile of droppings. There you may find your creature. Don't forget to check under leaves.

How to Catch Them

If you find a hornworm, just pluck it gently from the branch. It will not bite or sting. It will probably cling to the stem with its legs. Pull slowly and carefully so that you don't injure it. Put it in a container with a stem and leaves of the plant where you found it.

How to Keep Them

Any caterpillar needs fresh leafy stems from its food plants twice daily. In this case, the food plants are those in the tomato family: tomato, tobacco, potato, pepper, eggplant, and petunia. If it does not eat the first leaves you offer, try a different plant in this group. Your hornworm will be able to eat the leaves more easily if you give it a stem with leaves attached rather than plucked leaves. It's very important to change the leaves twice every day. Caterpillars cannot eat wilted or dried leaves. Spray the leaves every day with a few droplets of water.

A 12-by-7 inch (30 × 18-cm) terrarium is big enough. The caterpillar will spend most of its time on the leaves, so you don't need soil or sand on the floor of the terrarium.

Caterpillar waste (called **fras**) will fall to the floor of the terrarium if the hornworm is eating. It is in the form of small dry pellets. Dump the fras out every day or your caterpillar may get sick.

These caterpillars can become ready to pupate at 3 inches (8 cm) or 6 inches (15 cm) or anywhere in between. If your friend is this size and stops eating, or begins wandering around the terrarium restlessly for several hours (even though it has fresh leaves), then it may be ready to pupate or metamorphose.

Tomato Hornworm pupa

To get the terrarium ready for the caterpillar to pupate, put in at least 4 inches (10 cm) of loose soil or potting soil. It should be slightly damp—not bone dry, but definitely not soggy. When the caterpillar feels the urge, it will burrow down into the soil and shed its skin. Underneath will be a new skin that hardens into a sort of shell, like a cocoon. Your pet is no longer a caterpillar, but a pupa. The pupa is brown, about 2 inches (5 cm) long, and has an odd structure on its front that looks like a jug handle. In this stage it will stay underground all winter. While it is waiting for spring, the little creature inside the pupal skin becomes a beautiful moth.

When May or June arrives, the adult moth crawls out of the pupal skin and up to the surface of the soil. It pumps blood into its wet, crumpled wings. The wings begin to straighten out and dry.

If an adult moth emerges from the soil in your terrarium, you must let it go free as soon as its wings are straight and it begins trying to fly. It will damage its wings beating them against the sides of the terrarium. You can let the moth cling to your finger for a moment before you release it. This won't hurt it as long as you don't touch its wings.

When you release it, put it in a sheltered place such as under a bush, in case it is not quite ready to fly. A sitting butterfly or moth is easy prey for a bird or a mouse.

What They Act Like

The adult moths are usually called hawkmoths, because of the narrow pointed shape of their wings and their smooth, swift flight, like that of a hawk.

The scientific name of the family is Sphingidae, after the famous structure in Egypt called the Sphinx. They are also commonly called sphinx moths. When resting, the caterpillar holds itself a little like the Sphinx, with the front part of the body raised and the smooth head pulled in a little.

Five-Spotted Hawkmoth

Yet another name is used for some of these moths. Some are called hummingbird moths, from their method of feeding. They are able to hover in front of a flower just as hummingbirds do. And like hummingbirds, the adult moths drink nectar from flowers. They have a long tubular mouthpart called a **proboscis,** which stays coiled up when not in use. As they hover in front of a flower, the proboscis uncoils. It probes deep inside the flower to reach the nectar, a sugary fluid produced by the flower.

There's one more thing about hornworms that I have to mention. You may see one that has some odd little white things glued to its back, little things that look like the tips of cotton swabs, but much smaller. They are tiny white cocoons. If your hornworm has them, it will die before it becomes a pupa.

The cocoons are from a very small type of wasp called a braconid wasp. The adults are only $\frac{1}{16}$ to $\frac{5}{8}$ inch (2 to 15 mm) in length. The female wasp lays her eggs on the skin of a hornworm. When the eggs hatch, the larvae burrow through the skin into the caterpillar's insides. There, they feed on the caterpillar's body fluids. At first the caterpillar carries on almost normally. But then it gets weaker and weaker. The wasp larvae eat and grow, then they burrow back through the skin to the outside and make cocoons on the caterpillar's back. I have often seen 30 to 50 cocoons on the back of a single hornworm, but some have many more than that, maybe hundreds. The caterpillar may die before the adult wasps emerge from their cocoons. Gardeners like braconid wasps because they help keep the number of hornworms down. And that's good for tomato plants.

Carolina Sphinx

Your pet caterpillar will be safer from egg-laying braconid wasps if you keep a cloth over its cage. These tiny wasps can easily go through the openings in most cage lids, but not through cloth.

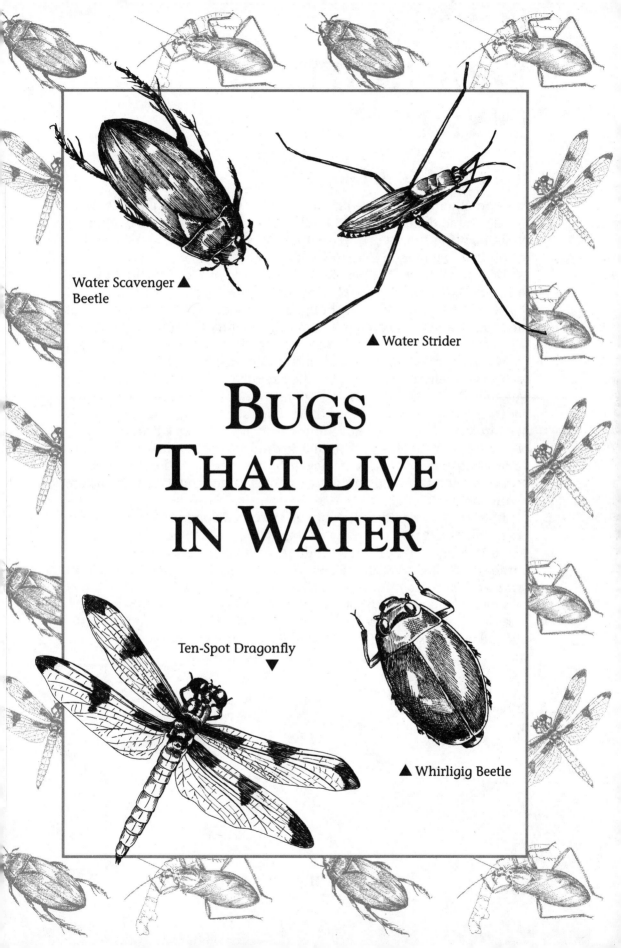

Water Scavenger ▲
Beetle

▲ Water Strider

BUGS
THAT LIVE
IN WATER

Ten-Spot Dragonfly
▼

▲ Whirligig Beetle

DRAGONFLY ——————— NYMPHS

What They Look Like

As a group, dragonflies are among the oldest of our flying insects. They first appeared about 280 to 350 million years ago, in the Carboniferous period. During those early years there was a type of dragonfly with a wingspan of more than 2 feet (60 cm)!

Nowadays, they're not so big. They range from ¾ to 5 inches long (18 to 127 mm). They are very easy to recognize with very long slim abdomens that stick way out behind, and bulging compound eyes that cover most of the head. The wings of dragonflies may be their most distinctive trait. The wings are more or less clear, or membranous, but they may be tinted. And the wings have veins all through them that you can easily see.

You can tell dragonflies from their relatives, the damselflies, by the way they hold their wings. Dragonflies cannot fold their wings over the body as most insects do. At rest their wings stick straight out to the side, like airplane wings. They have four wings, and the back two are a little bigger. Damselflies look very similar to dragonflies, but their eyes are not quite as big and their wings are held together over the abdomen, pointing backward, at rest. Also a damselfly is more slender and its four wings are all the same size.

In North America there are about 450 species of dragonflies, so there are a wide variety of color patterns. Many are green, blue, or red.

Since dragonflies undergo gradual metamorphosis, immature dragonflies are called nymphs. They are also sometimes called naiads. In some ways the dragonfly nymphs look like their parents. They have bulgy eyes and a long abdomen, but their eyes don't cover most of their heads. And like all nymphs, they lack wings. At all stages of the dragonfly's life, the abdomen is segmented, looking like a series of rings stacked on a pole. This segmentation is especially easy to see in the nymph.

It might surprise you to hear that dragonfly nymphs live in water,

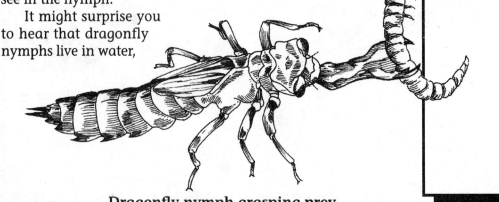

Dragonfly nymph grasping prey

Aquatic net

even though the adults live on land. Many other animals follow this same pattern of moving from water to land as they become adults. Some examples are mayflies, stoneflies, mosquitoes, and many species of frogs, toads, and salamanders.

How do you tell a dragonfly nymph from a damselfly nymph? A damselfly nymph has three leaflike gills sticking out of the tip of its abdomen. A dragonfly nymph doesn't.

Where to Find Them

Adult males can be found near the edges of ponds, perching on stumps, sticks, reeds, logs, or rocks. They stay at the pond through the middle part of the day. Females may be found more often away from ponds, but will visit a pond to mate and lay eggs. Since dragonflies are fast fliers, you may see them in forests or fields or yards well away from ponds.

To find a nymph, look in shallow water along the edges of ponds and lakes, especially near vegetation. Always take an adult with you when looking in or near a body of water.

How to Catch Them

Because dragonflies are large and spend a lot of time in flight, they will not be happy in a cage. But the nymphs or naiads can be happy as clams in a small aquarium.

To catch a nymph, try turning over dead leaves underwater, along the edges of ponds and lakes. You can also use a long-handled aquatic net, sometimes called a dip net, designed for use in water. You can order one

Ten-Spot Dragonfly

Phylum:	*Arthropoda (joint-legged animals)*
Class:	*Insecta (insects)*
Order:	*Odonata (dragonflies and damselflies)*
Family:	*Several*
Characteristics:	*Aquatic nymphs. Abdomen long or rounded, with obvious segmentation. Big eyes on a large head. Long, thin legs.*
Distribution:	*Throughout the United States*
Food:	*Insects, tadpoles, small fish*

from a biological supply company (see the Appendix), or if you have a science museum store or science hobby shop in your town, you might find one there. Bump the edge of the net lightly over the pond floor, touching down at intervals. This is a good way to catch critters, but you'll also gather a lot of leaves off the pond floor. Dump the whole mess into a white pan or a clear glass pan resting on a white piece of paper. The white background makes creatures much easier to see. Then pick through the leaves carefully, looking on both sides of each one. A nymph that is coated with mud blends in very well with wet muddy leaves. After you've looked at every leaf and put them one by one into a bucket, look in the water that's left in the dish.

If you see a long-legged, very segmented insect with an abdomen that gets wider toward the hind end, then you probably have a dragonfly nymph.

You can scoop up the nymph with a cup, or with a piece of cardboard. It may bite (not sting) if you annoy it or put your finger in its face, so be careful.

Carry the creature home in a container of pond water. Clear water is better than very muddy water, which tends to clog its gills. If you put a lid on the container, leave at least half the space filled with air. Then the water it is breathing can pick up fresh oxygen from the air. Don't leave the lid on tightly for more than an hour. If it's a long way home, lift the lid every once in a while and fan the inside of the jar to push fresh air in.

How to Keep Them

The nymph will need an aquarium about 10 to 12 inches (25 to 30 cm) long, with a thin (½-inch or 1-cm) layer of sand or soil on the bottom. Put no more than about 3 inches (8 cm) of water in the terrarium, so that oxygen circulating from the surface will reach the bottom. After you put the water in, it may take a week for the sand or soil to settle and the water to clear. If you haven't done it in advance, just leave out the sand or soil. Instead put a single layer of leaves from the pond floor. If you can't use pond water, you can use springwater (not distilled water) from a grocery store.

Nymphs of both dragonflies and damselflies will eat worms, the larvae of other insects, tadpoles, and small crustaceans such as amphipods and isopods. They will probably try to eat any small animal that moves and that doesn't eat them. Amphipods and isopods look sort of like half-grown pill bugs but they live in water. You can collect them from ditches or ponds by dragging a 4-by-6-inch (10 × 15-cm) goldfish net through underwater weeds. A goldfish net is much smaller and less sturdy than a dip net, but can be bought at a pet store.

An easy thing to try to feed your nymph is an earthworm, or a small caterpillar, although the caterpillar will not live long underwater. As the nymph grows larger it may eat very small fish. If you have more than one nymph in an aquarium, they may eat each other.

You will need to put in the aquarium a branch that sticks up out of the water, or a raft, that the nymph can cling to as its final molt occurs and its new wings unfurl.

What They Act Like

Dragonflies are predators. Predators have different styles of hunting. Spiders make traps, which we call webs. Then they sit quietly and wait. Mantises do a lot of sitting and waiting, too, relying on their camouflage to keep them hidden from their prey. When a fly or moth comes close enough, the mantis grabs it. (See my earlier book, *Pet Bugs,* John Wiley & Sons, 1994, for more on mantises.)

How do dragonflies go about catching their prey? Dragonflies are more like wolves or hawks. They don't rely on camouflage. They go after their prey. Some species fly back and forth near the pond looking for prey. Others sit on their perches, waiting for some poor sap to wander by. Then, *bam!* The dragonfly grabs the prey with its long, hairy legs, in midair, then curves its legs around the prey like a basket. Still flying, the dragonfly cuts up the prey with its sharp jaws and eats it. The prey could be any flying insect, but dragonflies eat a lot of mosquitoes and flies.

Like mantises, dragonflies can turn their heads back and forth as they search. Most insects can't do this. Being able to look around freely is a great advantage to a predator that doesn't have a trap.

A nymph is just as terrible as the adult, if you happen to be pea-size prey. Maybe more so. The youngster doesn't simply grab its prey and chew like its parents do. Its methods are more nightmarish. When it sees a lunch item, its mouth does a complete transformation. The nymph does not leap forward to grab the prey, but its mouth leaps forward instead! While its body stays in one place, the nymph uncovers, unfolds, and hurls forward an odd pair of pincers. The pincers seize the prey, bring it back to the mouth, and chew it up.

When a nymph is ready to become an adult, it crawls up a stem or anything sticking out of the water. It gets a good grip and then makes some odd movements that stretch the skin on its back. The skin splits. The adult dragonfly crawls out and clings to the empty skin. At first its wings are crumpled and wet. Then blood is pumped into the veins in its wings, which causes them to straighten out. As soon as the wings harden, the dragonfly is ready to go.

Damselfly

WHIRLIGIG BEETLES

What They Look Like

Whirligigs are small, oval, black beetles about ½ inch (12 mm) long that live in water. Their behavior is very peculiar. They whirl around on the surface of ponds and streams, going first one way and then another. Often they skate in clusters that may be several feet across, each one spinning and changing directions constantly. This behavior makes them very easy to identify.

But even out of water, their bodies are still easy to recognize. Several features separate them from the other aquatic beetles. First of all, they have two sets of compound eyes that meet right at the surface of the water. The upper pair can see above water, the lower pair sees underwater. They need both sets of eyes because they have enemies both above and below the surface.

Their legs are unique, too. They have very long front legs that extend forward. These front legs are helpful in capturing and eating prey. While biting prey on the surface, whirligigs may push back or from side to side with their front legs, as dogs will use their legs to push away from you while pulling at a rag with their teeth.

The four back legs are much shorter, flat and wide and fringed with hair to help them work like paddles. The whirligigs' antennae are short and clublike.

Some species of whirligigs give off an odor of pineapples or apples when handled.

Many types of aquatic beetles come to the surface for air. But whirligigs are the only beetles that spend most of their time with the whole body floating on the surface.

Where to Find Them

Look for groups of whirligig beetles on the surface of streams, rivers, ponds, or lakes, usually near shore or in a sheltered spot. They are most abundant in late summer or early fall. Always take an adult with you when looking in or near a body of water.

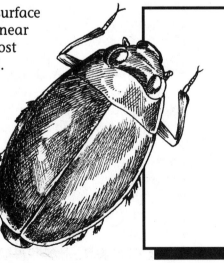

Adult whirligig beetle

How to Catch Them

You'll find it very hard to catch an individual that you may have singled out. For one thing, whirligigs are fast. Second, their constant zigzagging makes it very difficult to tell where an individual will be in the next second. And third, if whirligigs are disturbed, they may dive. They swim as well underwater as on the surface.

Your best bet is to go after a group of whirligigs. For this you'll need a long-handled aquatic net, sometimes called a dip net. Quickly sweep the dip net through the whirling beetles. Some will dive and some will swim crookedly away, but you may get a few.

Ideally your jar for taking the beetles home will have some water in it, some air, and perhaps a vertical twig wedged in place for the beetles to crawl on. But either a dry jar or a jar partially filled with water and no stick will do for a short period.

Be careful in transferring beetles from net to jar. These guys can fly and may take off. Keep a lid on the jar until you get them home to an aquarium.

How to Keep Them

You'll need an aquarium at least 12 by 7 inches (30 × 18 cm). A 10-gallon (38-liter) aquarium is better (about 20 by 10 inches or 51 × 25 cm). Fill the aquarium about half or three-fourths full with water from where you caught the beetles. If that is not possible, you can use springwater from the grocery (not distilled water).

Whirligigs like to climb out of the water and dry out occasionally. You can keep a stick wedged into the aquarium so that it's partly in and partly out of the water. If you add a small raft, they can climb on top for airing.

Phylum:	*Arthropoda (joint-legged animals)*
Class:	*Insecta (insects)*
Order:	*Coleoptera (beetles)*
Family:	*Gyrinidae (whirligig beetles)*
Characteristics:	*Usually in groups on the surface of the water, swimming fast in circles like a bunch of crazy motorboat drivers. Oval and shiny black. Two long front legs, back legs short.*
Distribution:	*Mostly in the eastern United States*
Food:	*Adults eat live prey or dead matter. Larvae prey on insect larvae in water.*

Make sure a wood raft is old weathered wood that will not leak chemicals into the water.

Whirligigs are predators. They will eat aquatic insects or insects that fall on the surface. Or they will eat meat that you offer. Try hanging a small sliver of cooked chicken at the water's surface. You can also toss onto the surface a cricket or moth, dead or alive, and watch what happens. Clean out any remaining morsels after a day or less. They may foul the water.

What They Act Like

The whirling action of whirligigs is the oddest thing about them. They've had many nicknames based on this behavior, such as waltzing beetles, writes-my-name beetles, scuttle bugs, and of course, whirligigs. Even their family name, Gyrinidae, comes from the word *gyrate,* which means "to move in a circular path."

Why do whirligigs do this? If you've tried to catch them, you may already know. Whirligigs are in much more danger of predation than are diving beetles or water scavenger beetles that stay underwater. Surface

**Group of whirligig beetles
on pond surface**

dwellers are *much* easier to spot than bottom dwellers or insects that cling to plants. Frogs as well as herons and other birds may eat them from above. Raccoons would, if they could catch them. From below, fish are a big danger. Many fish eat insects on the surface. Also turtles, water snakes, salamanders, and aquatic mammals like muskrats may eat these beetles in the water.

Whirligigs are easy to see. But the whirling behavior makes it hard for fish to take careful aim. A species of nonwhirling whirligigs would probably soon be eaten to extinction.

Whirligigs have other defenses against fish, too. If they detect fish in the water, whether a live fish or a tiny piece of raw fish you've put in the aquarium, they will either dive, or crawl out of the water.

Whirligigs may seem to be swimming about randomly, but they're not. They don't bump into each other unless they mean to. They can detect tiny waves in the water that tell them when something is ahead. They also make tiny sounds that bounce off of objects ahead, much the same as bats and porpoises do. This method of locating objects is called **echolocation.**

But sometimes they bump on purpose. One whirligig may circle another one, swim figure eights around it, sideswipe it, and even ram it straight on. I don't know why they do this.

They may also charge water striders or other insects that they could eat. A surprise attack is more likely to be successful than a hesitant approach. Whirligigs sometimes swim full blast onto leaves where a fly could be resting. Any insect that falls onto the water surface is fair game, even one much bigger than the whirligig. They will attack in groups, each one jerking itself, first left, then right, until a hunk of meat comes away— rather like a group of African hunting dogs or hyenas eating a fallen antelope.

WATER SCAVENGER BEETLES

What They Look Like

Water scavenger beetles are small beetles that spend most of their time in water, eating plants in the shallow edges of ponds and lakes. Most are black, smooth, and shiny, but they can be brown, dull green, or yellow. Their shape is oval, with a rounded back and a flattened belly. Each beetle carries on its belly a layer of air for breathing, which gives the underside a shimmery, silver look. There are over 200 species of water scavenger beetles, ranging in length from $\frac{1}{16}$ to $1\frac{1}{2}$ inches (1 to 40 mm) long.

The antennae of water scavenger beetles are important in telling them apart from another family of water beetles, the predaceous diving beetles. The water scavenger's antennae are short and shaped like clubs. In between the antennae are two long skinny mouthparts that can look like antennae if the true antennae are tucked out of sight. These mouthparts are called maxillary palps. In the water scavenger family, the maxillary palps are longer than the antennae. Predaceous diving beetles have long, threadlike antennae that are longer than the maxillary palps.

Like many other aquatic beetles, water scavenger beetles often have back legs that are flattened and fringed with hair, so the legs can work like paddles or flippers. Another important thing to observe for identification is that water scavengers move their legs alternately. First right, then left, then right, and so on. The look-alike predaceous diving beetles move the legs on both sides at the same time, like one person using two oars.

Some water scavenger beetles have a sort of spine at the hind end of the body. And some have a keel on the underside, which keeps the body from turning side to side when the legs alternate kicks.

Here's another way water scavengers are different from predaceous diving beetles: water scavengers come to the surface headfirst to gather more air, while the predaceous diving beetles come to the surface hind end first.

**Adult water
scavenger beetle**

Where to Find Them

Look in shallow areas of ponds, lakes, and streams, especially in vegetation. Always take an adult with you when looking in or near a body of water. The adult beetles may fly to porch lights or lanterns at night.

How to Catch Them

Use a long-handled aquatic net to sweep through vegetation along the edges of ponds or lakes, especially in stagnant areas. You may be able to see the beetles coming to the surface for air. After you've swept the pond weeds or pond surface with the net, dump the contents into a clean bucket or pan. Predaceous diving beetles and giant water bugs (which may be mistaken for beetles) may bite, so scoop up any beetles you want with a spoon or piece of cardboard. Put them into a carrying jar half full of water. If you'll be traveling less than an hour, you can put a lid tightly on the jar. For longer periods, remove the lid and fan the air inside the jar periodically.

How to Keep Them

Water scavengers are easy to keep in an aquarium. Use one at least 12 by 7 inches (30 × 18 cm), or better, a 10-gallon (38-liter) glass aquarium. Fill the aquarium to within a couple of inches of the top with water from the pond where you collected the beetles. If that's impossible, use springwater from the grocery or tap water that has been left standing open to the air for 24 to 48 hours, long enough for the chlorine to evaporate. The beetles will be breathing air, so you won't need a pump to aerate the water. You won't need a filter either.

Add to the pond a few leaves or rocks from a stream or pond that have a slick coating of algae. (If they feel slippery, that's algae.) Add a couple of

Phylum:	*Arthropoda (joint-legged animals)*
Class:	*Insecta (insects)*
Order:	*Coleoptera (beetles)*
Family:	*Hydrophilidae (water scavenger beetles)*
Characteristics:	*Oval-shaped, most are black or dark green and shiny. Underside covered with a silvery coating of air when underwater. Come to the surface head-first. Kick back legs alternately when swimming.*
Distribution:	*Throughout the United States*
Food:	*Adults are scavengers, larvae are predators.*

strands of some type of pond vegetation, too, with some living leaves and some decaying leaves. Anchor one end of the strands under a rock, or in a piece of clay if you can, so that the strands don't float entirely on the surface. If you can't find any pond weeds in a pond, look in a pet store that sells fish, or in a home supply store like Home Depot. Your beetles may enjoy a stick, too, for resting on, wedged in or tied to a stone on the bottom so that part of the stick is underwater and part of it is above water. Since water scavengers can fly, you'll need some kind of lid. Use one that lets air circulate.

Water scavengers occasionally eat meat. You can try offering cooked egg. Fry an egg on a nonstick pan with no grease. Cut a small strip and hang it on a thread in the water. Or you can hang a very small piece of raw beef on a thread in the water. Don't leave the meat or egg in the water longer than a few hours, or it will begin to foul the water. Too much decaying vegetation will also make the water smell bad. Keep the aquarium in a place where it doesn't get more than an hour of direct sunlight.

Your water scavenger beetle will enjoy a small raft made of weathered wood or something else with a rough texture that floats. Don't use new wood, which may release chemicals into the water. Since water scavengers are air breathers, you might think they would rest on top of the raft. But they prefer to rest *under* it, belly side up! A water scavenger has air stored on its body, which makes the beetle tend to float. Without a raft to hold it down, a water scavenger must either cling to something or kick continually to keep itself underwater. But the raft enables it to relax. The beetle may even take a bath under the raft, cleaning its head and body with its legs.

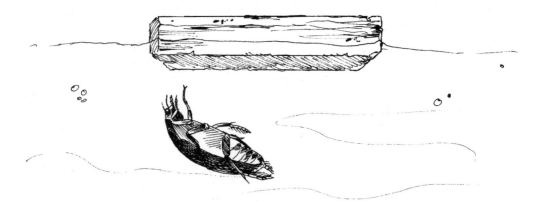

Water scavenger beetle returning to surface of water

What They Act Like

Porpoises and whales are mammals that breathe air but live underwater. They just come to the surface to breathe every once in a while, and then go for long periods underwater without breathing. Water scavenger beetles don't come to the surface to breathe. They come to the surface to replenish the air that is stored on their bodies. They breathe that stored air while they're underwater.

Part of the air is stored on the belly. But more air is trapped under the elytra (wing covers) on the beetle's curved back. Which air does the beetle breathe, and how? The water scavenger actually breathes the air under the elytra on the back. Insects have small openings called spiracles for breathing. The spiracles open into small tubes inside the body. A water scavenger's spiracles are under its elytra. When the air under the elytra gets low in oxygen, the beetle makes a very interesting maneuver. The little creature opens its elytra just a bit, and using its hair-fringed back feet, it transfers some air from its back to its belly. The beetle now has not just a shimmery coating on the belly, but a big bulge of air. The water scavenger combs this air bubble with the hair fringes on its back and middle legs. This gets rid of waste gases and lets in fresh oxygen from the water. Yes, water has dissolved oxygen in it; that's what fish breathe. When this is done, the beetle opens its elytra again, very slightly, and slips a good part of the air bubble back under them.

If a water scavenger refreshes its air supply with oxygen from the water, then why does it ever need to go to the surface? Eventually the volume of air in the beetle's bubble decreases as nitrogen from the bubble moves into the water. A bigger bubble is needed. So the beetle goes to the surface and uses its club-shaped antennae to gather new air. The antennae are hairy like the rear legs. The hair helps trap air. The water scavenger reaches up with one or both antennae, scoops a bit of air, and brings the air down into the silvery bubble on its belly. The beetle opens the elytra slightly at the same time, sucking some of the air up under them. This may be repeated several times in one trip to the surface.

WATER STRIDERS

What They Look Like

If you have spent any time around ponds or quiet streams, you have probably seen water striders. They are the most common of all the insects that live on the surface of the water. At first glance, they look a little like giant mosquitoes skating over the surface on their long, thin legs. But they are much too big to be mosquitoes, ranging in length from ⅜ to 1 inch (9 to 25 mm).

Most species have long, slender, dark brown or blackish bodies. Some are rounder in shape. They stand on the water with the tips of their four back legs, making small dents in the water's surface. The little dents often cast four little round shadows on the stream or pond bottom.

The two front legs are shorter and are held up off the water. They are used for capturing prey.

Water striders are true bugs, in the order Hemiptera. Like all hemipterans, Water Striders have at least a partial X pattern on the back, created by their closed wings.

Where to Find Them

Look on the surfaces of ponds and slow streams. Since most Water Striders are slim and only about ½ inch long, they are not easy to see when still. But motion makes them or their shadows easy to spot. Always take an adult with you when looking in or near a body of water.

How to Catch Them

Water striders have sensors on their feet that can feel even tiny vibrations in the water. So you will definitely not catch one by following it slowly around the surface with your dip net in the water. It will always feel the net coming and move the other way.

You may get one by moving the net very quickly, and by moving the net through air rather than water, at least until the last minute. Try to suddenly bring the net down into the water

Adult water strider

and up under the water strider. Use the edge of the net to slice through the water. If you bring it right down upon the water strider, you may well mangle and drown it.

For moving the strider to your aquarium, have a jar with some damp moss or a slightly crumpled damp paper towel (not sodden, and not wadded) in the bottom. Don't put the bug in a jar of water. These insects breathe air, and the sloshing in a jar of water might drown it.

Many water striders cannot fly, but some can. So get the strider into a jar as soon as you can. Cover the jar with a piece of cloth, held in place with a rubber band. For a short trip home, a plastic or metal jar lid is all right.

How to Keep Them

A water strider will need a good patch of surface area to be happy, so you'll need an aquarium that's at least 12 by 7 inches (30 × 18 cm). A 10-gallon (38-liter) aquarium is better. (This is the most commonly sold size of glass aquarium.) The depth of the water is not nearly as important as the surface area. Remember that water striders can fly, so keep the lid on at all times. It's best to keep water striders

Water striders on pond

Phylum:	*Arthropoda (joint-legged animals)*
Class:	*Insecta (insects)*
Order:	*Hemiptera (true bugs)*
Family:	*Gerridae (water striders)*
Characteristics:	*Thin body and long legs. Looks like a big mosquito. Skates on the surface of the water.*
Distribution:	*Throughout the United States*
Food:	*Small insects*

just during the warmer part of the year, because during the winter many hibernate under leaves or logs on the shore, or even under logs on the bottom of the pond.

Feed your water strider other insects by dropping the prey on the water. You can catch small insects with a sweep net by sweeping the net through tall grass. Or you can look under a log or board to catch a small cricket. You may be able to catch a small moth by turning on a porch light at night. A single prey item once a day or every other day is plenty.

What They Act Like

How do water striders stand on water without sinking? Lots of insects float on the surface because of **surface tension**. This does not mean that there is really a film on top of the water. Water molecules all have a slight electrical charge on each end. Because of these charges, the water molecules are attracted to each other. They behave as though they are weakly joined together by this attraction. When something presses on the water molecules from above, they remain stuck together and the surface bends. But it will only bend so far, then the molecules separate and the object punctures the surface.

A sharp object will poke through the surface much more easily than a wide object. Water striders have hairs on the tips of their legs that make the tips wider, so that their legs won't puncture the surface. To glide around, they push against the water with their middle legs, dragging their back legs behind them.

The sensors on water striders' legs help them catch their prey. When a small insect falls on the surface, its struggles make vibrations or tiny waves. The sensors tell the water strider which direction the movement is coming from. The water strider glides toward the prey. When the prey is close enough, the strider may leap into the air and pounce on its victim. It grabs the prey with its front legs, and stabs the struggling creature with its sharp beak. The water strider injects substances into the prey to partly digest it, and then sucks out the resulting fluids. But don't worry, water striders don't bite humans.

The male is good at making vibrations as well as feeling them. When he is ready to mate, he attracts a female by using his legs to make a particular pattern of vibrations on the water. These vibrations may also warn other males to stay away.

After they mate, the female lays her eggs on stones or other objects sticking out of the water. The male stands guard to make sure no one bothers her. The eggs hatch into small nymphs that look just like the parents, but smaller.

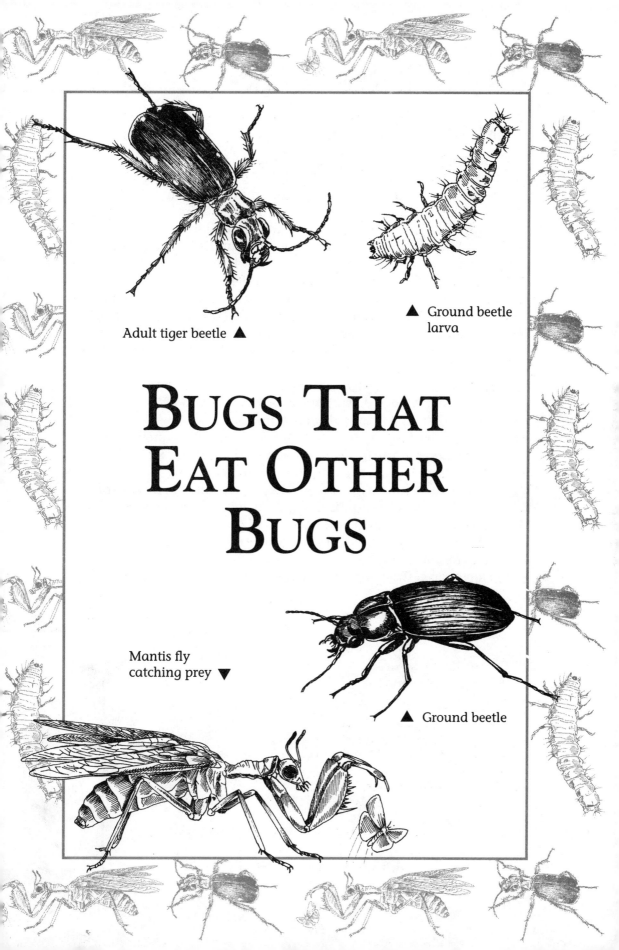

Adult tiger beetle ▲

▲ Ground beetle larva

BUGS THAT EAT OTHER BUGS

Mantis fly catching prey ▼

▲ Ground beetle

MANTIS FLIES _____

What They Look Like

A mantis fly is not the same thing as a praying mantis. The first time I saw a mantis fly I was really puzzled. It looked like a praying mantis, but it was less than an inch long, much too small to be a mantis. Mantises can be small when they are immature, of course, but immature ones have no wings. This creature had wings, and they didn't look like mantis wings. They looked like the wings of an adult ant lion or lacewing—clear, with netlike veins. (You can read about ant lions and lacewings in my earlier book, *Pet Bugs,* John Wiley & Sons, 1994.)

It turned out that the little insect was a mantis fly, or mantispid. They are named after the mantises they look like, but are not closely related to mantises at all. Rather they are in the order Neuroptera, which also includes ant lions, lacewings, and other net-winged insects. All have clear wings with netlike veins as adults. The wings when closed are not flat on the back like beetles' wings or mantises' wings. Rather they come together to make a rooflike ridge down the back. There are two pairs of wings, all similar in size. All are long and oval-shaped.

The first pair of legs of the mantis fly are for grabbing prey. They come off of the long **prothorax** (front section of the thorax) just behind the head. These front legs, in both mantis flies and mantises, are large, heavily muscled, and lined with spikes. They're responsible for most of the action. All the legs of a mantis fly, and the location of the legs, are very much like those of a praying mantis.

Both mantis flies and mantises have triangular faces—a pointed mouth at the bottom corner with chewing mouthparts, and two large eyes at the top corners. The large eyes are for spotting prey.

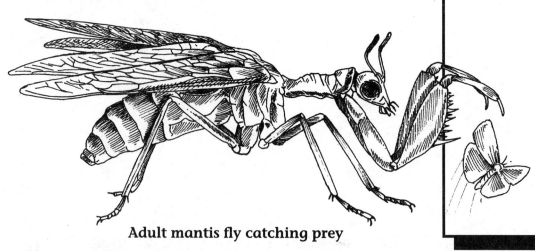

Adult mantis fly catching prey

Adult mantis flies range from ¾ to 1 inch (20 to 25 mm) in length, including the wings. The wings extend well beyond the end of the body. Adult praying mantises are *much* larger, from 2½ to 4 inches (6 to 10 cm) in length, including wings. In some mantis species, the wings are shorter than the body. In some, the wings are the same length.

Mantis flies can be green, brown, or yellow and black. The ones I've seen have all been green.

There is a type of mantis fly, in the genus *Climaciella,* that looks like a small wasp. These are brown or black and many have yellow bands. This mimicry may be a form of protection from predators. Many insects mimic other insects that sting, are poisonous, or just taste bad.

Where to Find Them

Mantis flies live in the edges of wooded areas and in fields or grasslands. But the mantis flies that I have caught have all been in or on my house. I live in a suburban area, with a school athletic field and small wooded areas nearby. I have probably been near dozens of mantis flies in nature, but they are so well camouflaged that I notice them only on artificial structures, such as walls, where they don't blend in. You've probably been near lots of them, too. Now that you know what they look like, maybe you'll be able to spot one.

How to Catch Them

Catching a mantis fly is not difficult. They fly, but they're not especially quick. If you see one on a wall, put a jar over it. Then slide a piece of paper or thin cardboard between the jar and the wall. Be careful not to crush the insect against the inside of the jar. If the mantis fly is on a leaf,

Phylum:	*Arthropoda (joint-legged animals)*
Class:	*Insecta (insects)*
Order:	*Neuroptera (net-winged insects)*
Family:	*Mantispidae (mantis flies)*
Characteristics:	*Look like praying mantises with strong, spiky front legs for grasping. Wings clear with netlike veins, folded over the back like the peak of a roof.*
Distribution:	*Throughout the United States except for the Northwest, more common in the South*
Food:	*Adults eat insects and other small prey. Larvae are parasitic in the egg sacs of wandering spiders.*

put the jar over the leaf and insect from above. Cover the opening with the jar lid, breaking off the leaf and leaving it inside the jar. A lid with no holes is okay for an hour or two, but after that you'll need to poke airholes in the lid or replace it with a cloth lid. Remember not to leave the jar in direct sunlight or in a hot car.

How to Keep Them

Keep the mantis fly in a jar. You can put a lightweight twig in the jar for the mantis fly to rest on, although your creature can easily rest on the plastic side of the jar instead. It does not need soil or sand or stones or grass in the bottom of the jar. For a lid, use a piece of cloth held in place with a rubber band.

To offer water, spray the inside of the jar once a day with a plant mister or sprayer, just enough to put a few droplets inside the jar. If you don't have a sprayer, just flick a few droplets in with your fingers. Don't put water in a small dish inside the jar. It will probably slosh out and drown the mantis fly. Insects rarely drink from dishes; they prefer droplets, because in nature they often drink dew droplets.

Mantis flies I've kept have eaten fruit flies. You can trap fruit flies in warm weather by setting a baited jar on its side in a shady outdoor area, near a garbage can. Bait the jar with half a grapefruit rind (edible part not necessary), a banana peel, or two apple cores. Move it to a new location if you don't get any fruit flies after five days or so. Once you see flies inside, creep very slowly toward the jar, and slap the lid on the jar very quickly.

Put the whole jar in the freezer for about 60 seconds. The cold will paralyze the fruit flies temporarily. If they are still moving after 60 seconds in the freezer, check them every 15 seconds until they are all lying still. Take the jar out then, or they may freeze completely and die. While the fruit flies are chilled and paralyzed, quickly open the jar and put several small flies in with your mantis fly. You can move them with your fingers or with a small paintbrush.

If you can't catch any fruit flies, try any small insect or spider. If the mantis fly doesn't like it, try something else. Keep in mind the size of the mantis fly's front legs and keep the prey small. Some small insects, such as sow bugs, millipedes, and some beetles, protect themselves by tasting bad, so keep trying new things if your first offerings are rejected.

What They Act Like

Like praying mantises, mantis flies have evolved body parts that are specialized for catching prey. The mantis fly's large eyes spot the prey, then its head turns to watch it. The length of the prothorax and the long front legs make it easier for the mantis fly to grab the prey. The four back legs are just right for balancing the body while the insect lunges at the prey. But the most specialized of all these body parts are the spiky, strong front legs.

Mantis flies ambush their prey. This means that they sit still and wait, rather than hunt. If a fly or other small creature lands nearby, the mantis fly takes a few steps toward it, then reaches out and snatches it in the time it takes you to blink. The prey is squeezed and pierced with the spikes inside the front legs. There is no escape. And while the prey is held, it is eaten alive.

Mantis flies hatch from tiny eggs that are attached by short stalks to plants. Some of the larvae are smaller than $\frac{1}{16}$ inch (less than 1 mm). And they are fast. They hustle around searching for . . . a spider! The larvae are **parasites** (animals that survive by feeding on other animals without killing them). They ride around on spiders, sucking the spiders' blood as they ride. If the spider giving the larva a ride is a male spider, the mantis fly larva will need to transfer to a female when the spiders mate.

When the female spider lays her eggs, the mantis fly larva crawls into the spider's egg sac and begins to eat the spider's eggs. With this feast, the larva becomes plump, slow, and grublike. Then it makes a silken cocoon inside the egg sac. Inside the cocoon it metamorphoses into an adult mantis fly. The adult chews through the cocoon and the spider egg sac, and flies away in search of prey and a mate.

Adult praying mantis

TIGER BEETLES

What They Look Like

Some adult tiger beetles look like spots of metallic green, flying so fast that it's hard to get a good look. The larva is another story. It is a drab and homely little creature, who looks not at all like its parents. It is a big-headed, fat, and pasty worm!

In the United States there are several species of tiger beetles that look quite different from one another. Some are one color all over—green, blue, bronze, purple, or orange—while some have patterned wing covers (elytra). The patterns can be reddish brown or beige, or other colors. On most, the head is shiny and metallic. For many, the elytra are also shiny and metallic. Adults range in size from $\frac{3}{8}$ to $\frac{7}{8}$ inch (10 to 21 mm) long.

Scarab beetles can also be shiny and metallic. But scarab beetles (including Green June Beetles and Japanese Beetles) are slow and awkward, while tiger beetles are very fast runners. Also the antennae are different. All scarab beetles have shortish antennae that resemble golf clubs, but tiger beetles have long, thin, knobless antennae, two-thirds as long as the body. Scarab beetles are rounder; tiger beetles are slimmer.

Other look-alikes are the carabids or ground beetles, which can have a metallic sheen. Carabids are fast, too. But they hide during the day, while tiger beetles love the sun. You are most likely to see tiger beetles on warm sunny days, sitting right out in the open on dry soil or on a beach.

Although the adult tiger beetles vary in appearance, the larval burrows or tunnels are all similar. The tunnel looks like someone poked a pencil straight down into the ground and then pulled it out. The ground around the tunnel is perfectly flat and undisturbed. The tunnels are often in sandy soil.

The larva looks in part like any beetle grub or larva— a long, fat, segmented, wormlike creature, sort of like a whitish caterpillar, but hairless and without the prolegs that a caterpillar has along the rear half of its body. Beetle larvae do have three pairs of true legs arising from the first three segments of the body.

Adult tiger beetle

The tiger beetle larva has an extra appendage that most beetle larvae lack. On its fifth abdominal segment (the abdomen begins after the third pair of legs), it has curved hooks that dig into the side of its burrow to keep it from being pulled out. You will never find the larva outside of its burrow. All you will see of the creature is the flat top of its head.

Where to Find Them

The adult tiger beetle lays her eggs on the ground, one at a time and widely spread. When the egg hatches into a tiny larva, the larva burrows right into the soil. The burrow is easy to recognize. It is a pencil-size hole, in hard-packed bare ground, with no piles of soil or any disturbance around it. The burrows of those species that live on beaches are often in the shade of the scattered plants that grow on beaches. The larva of the Six-Spotted Green Tiger Beetle is more likely to have its burrow along a shady path, or near a stream in dry, hard-packed sandy soil, or along relatively undisturbed roadsides.

Some big earthworms have pencil-size burrows. But earthworm burrows are usually in loose rich soil, not hard-packed sandy soil. And earthworm burrows usually have piles of castings around them (crumbled-looking soil that has passed through the earthworm's body) beside the burrow.

Phylum:	*Arthropoda (joint-legged animals)*
Class:	*Insecta (insects)*
Order:	*Coleoptera (beetles)*
Family:	*Cicindelidae (tiger beetles)*
Genus and species:	*Cicindela sexguttata (Six-Spotted Green Tiger Beetle), and others*
Characteristics:	*Wide head with bulging eyes, narrow middle, and wide abdomen covered with wings that are often nearly parallel at their sides. Legs long and slender. Color is blue, green, black, orange, or patterned, some iridescent. Fast and agile fliers that quickly take off when approached.*
Distribution:	*Throughout the United States, often in open sunny areas. The Six-Spotted Green Tiger Beetle is in the eastern United States.*
Food:	*Small insects and spiders*

Adults of some species are most often seen on beaches—shores of oceans, lakes, or streams. Some blend in with the sand. The adult Six-Spotted Green Tiger Beetle is most often seen along sandy paths.

How to Catch Them

The adults are almost impossible to catch by hand. Besides, they may pinch you with their jaws, so I don't recommend trying.

Catching the larva involves some trickery. Once it sees you approaching, it will duck out of sight into its burrow. You must wait quietly by the burrow, keeping low, until it comes back to the top. When it comes back, you will see the top of its head, which looks flat and shield-shaped. It's not as easy to see the hole when its head is in place, because the head is sand-colored. When you see the larva has come back to the top, you must move lightning fast to cut off its retreat, by jabbing a shovel or garden trowel into the ground underneath the larva, cutting through its burrow. Or you can get a grown-up to use a pick, which can cut out a deep hunk of soil faster than a shovel.

Gently put the shovelful of soil on a newspaper to see if you captured the odd little grub. Hopefully you didn't cut it in half. If you see the creature on the newspaper, put some soil into your jar or bucket first, then scoop up the larva with your trowel, or pick it up with a gloved hand and put it on top of the soil. It may try to bite you, so keep your fingers away from its jaws.

How to Keep Them

A quart jar will work, although a gallon jar will be better. Or you can use a plastic bucket.

Fill the jar with damp sand to a depth of at least 5 inches (12 cm) and pack it smoothly. With a pencil, poke a hole all the way to the bottom of the jar. You must use damp sand because dry sand won't keep its shape, and the tunnel will collapse when you pull out the pencil.

Put the larva into the jar near the hole. It will find the hole and crawl in. Or you can put the larva hind end first into the hole. Be sure to keep the jar out of the sun.

After a day or so, if you leave the larva alone, it will come to the top and plug the hole with the shieldlike top of its head. Now comes the fun part—feeding it! Offer it caterpillars or worms, moths, flies, or other insects. See what it likes best.

Keep the sand in the jar slightly damp by drizzling no more than a spoonful of water onto the sand every few days. Don't put any water near the hole itself, or it may collapse.

What They Act Like

Like most predators, both adult and larval tiger beetles have the mouth-parts needed to bite. It's always a possibility that they will mistake some part of your flesh for prey and chomp on you. If you handle them, I suggest putting them on the back of your hand or on a palm that is open wide, without any bitable folds. Predatory insects with chewing mouth-parts (such as tiger beetles) are unlikely to bite a flat, tight surface, especially if they don't feel threatened.

When you feed the larva a small caterpillar, it will not come out of the burrow to get the prey. The larva is not good at walking on the ground. The caterpillar must come quite close to the hole to be captured. When the prey gets close to the hole, the larva lifts its flat head and opens its big jaws. If it grabs something big that struggles enough to pull it out of the burrow, the hooks on its fifth abdominal segment anchor it into the hole.

You might recognize the adult tiger beetle best by its habits. When you are walking along a sunny path or along a gully or ditch whose banks are bare and exposed, or maybe on a beach, you might see a Six-Spotted Green Tiger Beetle fly up off the ground about 5 feet (1.5 m) in front of you. It will fly ahead of you for a bit, then stop and land, as if waiting for you. When you get within 5 or 7 feet (1.5 to 2 m), the beetle is off again.

**Tiger beetle larva
in its burrow**

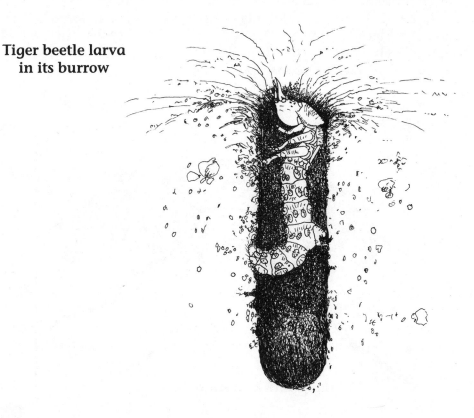

CARABID BEETLES ___
OR GROUND BEETLES

What They Look Like

The family Carabidae is one of the largest families of beetles, with over 3,000 species in North America. They are perhaps the most abundant beetles in the United States. But people who never garden or look under boards and logs may never see them. That's because most species of carabids come out only at night. Many of them hide by day in dark places— under rocks, boards, and so on.

Most species of carabids are all or partly black, a few are brightly colored. The body is usually shiny. The elytra are usually covered with parallel grooves running from front to back. The legs are nearly always long and slender, as compared to those of other beetles. Carabids have very narrow heads. The head at the eyes is always narrower than the pronotum, which is the covering over the thorax, just behind the head. In grasshoppers, the pronotum covers only the front part of the thorax. But a carabid's pronotum covers all of the top surface of the thorax.

All carabids are between ¹⁄₁₆ and 1⅜ inches (2 to 35 mm) in length, with most being between ³⁄₁₆ and ¾ inch (4 to 20 mm).

Some of the most commonly seen carabids under stones are the Common Black Ground Beetles in the genus *Pterostichus*. These small, shiny black beetles are ½ to ⅝ inch (13 to 16 mm) in length and, like most carabids, they have lengthwise grooves on their elytra.

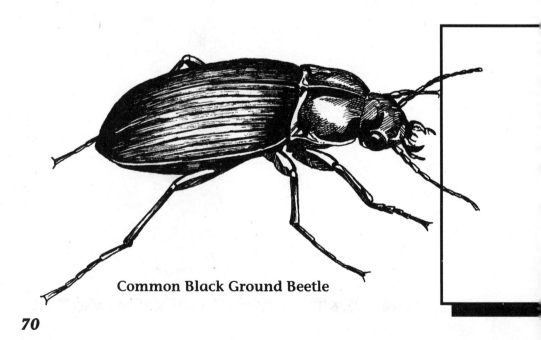

Common Black Ground Beetle

70

Another often-seen carabid is the Fiery Searcher, *Calasoma scrutator*. It is called "Fiery" because of the sheen of iridescent colors on its elytra. It is called "Searcher" because both adults and larvae climb trees in search of caterpillars to eat. This beetle is 1 to 1⅜ inches (25 to 36 mm) in length and mostly black, but the front of the thorax can have a bluish or violet tint. The elytra have a greenish metallic sheen with reddish edges. The Fiery Searcher also has lengthwise grooves along its elytra.

Another well-known group of ground beetles are the bombardier beetles, 40 species in the genus *Brachinus*. These have a narrow thorax, in addition to the narrow head that all ground beetles have. Many bombardier beetles are orange-tan all over, except for their bluish black elytra.

Where to Find Them

Most carabids are nocturnal. They come out only at night to pursue prey. But many, especially the Common Black Ground Beetles, can be found during the day under logs, boards, rocks, and leaves in moist areas, such as woods, gardens, and crop fields. You won't have much luck if the ground is dry.

If you see a half-inch-long black beetle under a rock or log, and if it runs away from you at lightning speed, then it's probably a carabid. But don't confuse carabids with wood roaches, which are similar in size, live in similar places, and are also fast. Carabids are mostly black, while wood roaches are brown, flattened, and have long, swept-back antennae.

Phylum:	*Arthropoda (joint-legged animals)*
Class:	*Insecta (insects)*
Order:	*Coleoptera (beetles)*
Family:	*Carabidae (ground beetles)*
Characteristics:	*Generally black and shiny, some colored. Head at eyes always narrower than the pronotum, the covering over the thorax. Legs long and slender. Very fast runners, usually under objects on the ground.*
Distribution:	*Throughout the United States*
Food:	*Caterpillars, beetle larvae, maggots, other insect larvae. Some species eat pollen, fungi, seeds, and decaying fruit.*

How to Catch Them

The easiest tool for catching a carabid is a large plastic peanut butter jar. You'll also need a square of cardboard big enough to cover the opening, and the plastic lid to the jar.

The procedure is easier if you have two people. One person flips the log or board, while the other holds the jar. Squat on the ground near the log or board, within arm's length of the spot where you think a beetle might be. Hold your jar upside down, lid off. Have your friend flip the board or log—away from you, so it's not in your way. If you kick or push the log before it's flipped, you will alert all the critters underneath it that you're coming and you'll probably find no one at home. So no one should touch the log or board until you're ready to roll, and then do it as quickly as possible.

If you see a black spot dashing away, clap the jar opening over it as fast as you can, so the beast is trapped on the ground. It will probably take you several tries to be able to do this. Once they've vanished into the leaf litter, they're probably gone for good.

But if you have trapped one in your jar, slide the piece of cardboard under the jar. Go slowly so the beetle can step up onto the cardboard. Once the cardboard is all the way under, flip the jar over and you've got it. Carabid beetles seldom fly. So while your captive is on the bottom of the jar, you can remove the cardboard and replace it with the lid for the trip home.

How to Keep Them

If you have only one or two beetles, a terrarium around 11 by 7 inches (28 × 18 cm) will work. Put about 2 inches (5 cm) of dark, damp loamy soil in the bottom of the terrarium. Loamy soil is like potting soil, with lots of decayed plant matter in it so that it is very dark brown and almost spongy. Pack it down, not hard, but firmly enough that it is more or less flat on top.

Put a big piece of bark flat over the surface of the soil. The ground beetles will probably stay under the bark and they may burrow into the soil. If you have a Fiery Searcher, prop up in the terrarium a branched stick or twig that it can climb.

Water your beetles with a plant mister every other day or so. Spray droplets on the side of the terrarium, low enough so the beetles can reach them. If you don't have a mister, use your fingers to flick some droplets against the side. Don't put a water dish in the terrarium. They won't drink from it and they might drown in it. Add a spoonful of water to the soil as needed to keep it slightly damp, but not soggy.

Most ground beetles eat other small animals, alive or dead. Offer them first of all soft, live insects like small caterpillars, maggots, and other insect larvae. Try also dead and dying insects. A few species of ground beetles eat seeds, pollen, berries, and decaying fruits and vegetables. Offer these if your captives are not interested in eating creatures.

What They Act Like

Ground beetles give the impression of being always frantic. They never walk calmly. They always move full speed ahead in a clumsy blundering way.

Common Black Ground Beetles have an interesting attraction to soil, or any dark cover. You can easily observe this attraction. Put a handful of damp, dark, loose soil in one corner of a terrarium or box, with the rest of the container bare. Then put a Common Black Ground Beetle in the terrarium. The beetle will rush at once into the pile of soil and bury itself. If you try to fish it out with a spoon, it will dive off the spoon back into the soil at once. The black color of its body blends in well, and it clings to the particles of soil so that it really is hard to see. Only the light reflecting off its shiny elytra gives it away.

Common Black Ground Beetles will make themselves right at home in a terrarium with slightly damp soil. If you put them into a terrarium with a 1-to-2-inch (24-to-48-mm) layer of soil in the bottom, they will immediately burrow into the soil and disappear. Over a period of a few days, they will each make a little burrow or chamber underground with a hole at the top. The hole may be as round as a pencil. You may be able to see a ground beetle moving around inside one of the burrows.

You can try making a couple of burrows for them before you put them into the terrarium. Put your finger into the soil up to the second knuckle. Your finger should not point straight down but should angle sideways. Pack the soil tightly around it, then pull your finger gently out, leaving a little burrow behind. Or you can do the same thing with the end of a pencil at an angle, instead of your finger.

Ground beetle larva

When you put the beetles into the terrarium, put one beetle directly into each burrow. Will they stay? The beetles may be more comfortable if you block out light by covering the burrows with a leaf or a piece of bark that's slightly curved so it doesn't lie flat against the soil.

They will come out at night, when the room is dark, to look for food. You may be able to catch them out and about if you creep up to the terrarium with a flashlight.

The ground beetles in the genus *Brachinus,* the bombardier beetles, have a very interesting mode of defending themselves. When threatened, these beetles lift their hind end and fire a chemical gas at the enemy. The gas is produced by secretions from glands in the beetle's hind end. When these secretions are mixed, they explode with a popping sound and a puff of vapor that can irritate skin. These beetles can fire up to six rounds in a row if necessary. If you come across a ground beetle that is orangish yellow all over except for bluish black elytra, use a cup to handle it.

You can appreciate how fast ground beetles are by racing them against other creatures that you find under rocks. Pill bugs are steady walkers that will put up a good race. But they always lose. Here's how you can compare the two. Put a piece of masking tape on a hard floor to mark the starting point. Place a single ground beetle on the tape, then use a kitchen timer or a stopwatch to measure the number of seconds that pass while the beetle walks in a straight line. As soon as the beetle stops or turns, stop the timer. Measure the distance. Divide seconds into inches to get the beetle's speed in inches per second. Do this with three beetles in all, each separately. Then repeat with three pill bugs. Who is faster? Do pill bugs have a means of defense other than running? Why do they roll into balls?

Adult crayfish ▼

▲ American
House Spider

BUGS
THAT AREN'T
INSECTS

▼ *Helix,* a garden snail

▲ Land planarian

AMERICAN HOUSE SPIDERLINGS

What They Look Like

Have you ever swept under a dresser and found a small spider skittering awkwardly about in your pile of dust? It was probably an American House Spider, the most common indoor spider. They are most easily recognized by their body shape and by the location and form of their web. Their webs are not like the familiar wheel-shaped webs with spokes that you see in Halloween drawings. The American House Spider's web is just a small irregular tangle of threads which often collects dust. This type of web is called a "cobweb." The house spider's cobwebs are often found in dark corners, or under something like a shelf or dresser that serves as a roof. Each spider hangs upside down and alone in its web, waiting for prey.

The body of an adult female house spider is about ¼ inch (5 to 6 mm) in length, not counting the legs. The body of a male is even smaller, at ⅛ to ¼ inch (3 to 6 mm). But most of the ones that you find indoors will be much smaller, with bodies as small as the head of a pin or smaller. The body might be about 1/16 inch (2 mm), with legs included ⅛ inch (3 mm). These little ones, the spiderlings, are the ones I like to keep as pets.

The bodies at all ages are yellowish brown with black-and-gray streaks and patches. The female's legs are yellow with black bands and the male's are orangish. The top of the female's rear body part (the abdomen) angles upward so sharply from the front body part (the **cephalothorax**) that her back appears humped.

The family of cobweb weavers includes other species besides the American House

American House Spider in its web

76

Spider. One of them has a shape and size very similar to the American House Spider's. It's the famous Black Widow. The adult female Black Widow has a poisonous bite. She is jet-black and shiny all over, except for the red hourglass on the underside of her abdomen. Black Widows are much less common than American House Spiders, and less likely to be indoors. But if you do happen to see one, don't touch it!

Where to Find Them

Sweeping is an excellent way to find American House Spiderlings. Their efforts to walk out of the debris pile make them easy to spot. But they are easy to find even without sweeping. Look behind and under desks, bookshelves, sofas—places Mom and Dad might forget to dust or vacuum. Look for a brownish motionless speck, suspended in midair.

If you can't find one, look in a friend's house whose parents are not as tidy as yours. Time of year makes no difference. Unlike Charlotte of *Charlotte's Web,* these spiders do not necessarily die in fall or winter. When kept warm indoors, they may survive all winter.

How to Catch Them

To capture an American House Spider that's on the floor, slide a sheet of paper under it, and lift it up. Bend the paper into a U-shape like a trough, and slide the spider into a small empty plastic jar, like a peanut butter jar. Cover the top of the bottle or jar with a lid that you've poked small holes in, or with a small piece of cloth held in place with a rubber band.

Another way to lift a spider off the floor is to drag your finger on the floor in a circle around the spider until you hit the silk line that is proba-

Phylum:	*Arthropoda (joint-legged animals)*
Class:	*Arachnida (spiders, mites, daddy longlegs, and others)*
Order:	*Araneae (spiders)*
Family:	*Theridiidae (cobweb weavers or comb-footed spiders)*
Genus and species:	Achaearanea tepidariorum
Characteristics:	*Hang upside down in corners of houses, in irregular, messy cobwebs. Yellowish brown body; abdomen streaked with black and brown.*
Distribution:	*Throughout the United States*
Food:	*Small insects*

bly still attached to the spider's hind end. Then you can lift the spider by the silk line like a yo-yo.

If the spider is suspended in its web, bring the jar or bottle up underneath it. Once you have the mouth of the jar up around the spider and its tiny web, use the lid or a piece of cardboard to trap it inside the jar. You can sometimes get a big part of the web in the jar, too, with the spider still in it. I've sometimes gotten very small American House Spiders this way without even disturbing them. They didn't seem to notice they'd been moved. The edges of the web that were clipped by the jar just stuck to the jar so that the web stayed intact. The web is just a jumble of threads, so it has no particular shape anyway.

Adult Black Widow in its web

In general, it is not a good idea to handle spiders unless you know what they are and that they won't bite. I don't know if an adult American House Spider will bite if handled roughly. It might, so don't handle adults. However, very young American House Spiderlings *cannot* bite, because their jaws are too small and weak to pierce your skin. So you can handle the very small ones freely. They are very clumsy in walking across your hand, because their legs are built for walking on threads.

Don't handle a spiderling whose body is any longer than $\frac{1}{16}$ inch (2 mm), to be sure there's no possibility of being bitten. Black Widow spiderlings are orange, white, and black when very young and could possibly be mistaken for American House Spiderlings. The amount of black on the bodies of Black Widows increases as they mature.

How to Keep Them

The spider will build a small web inside the jar, even if it is only as big as a baby food jar. The little creature will attach the threads to the side of the jar. The only thing you might possibly want to put inside the jar with the spider is a branched twig, but only if you can wedge it in place so that it doesn't shift around when you move the jar. If it moves, take it out.

Don't put grass, leaves, sand, or pebbles in the jar. The spider doesn't need them. Anything that moves around in the jar will destroy its web. A moving object may also kill the spider, and will provide a hiding place for its prey. Your pet will not need water if it is fed regularly. You may want to spray the web occasionally with a fine mist, but this isn't necessary. I have never seen a house spider drink water.

I have five American House Spiderlings now, which I have discovered during the last three months. Each lives alone in a clear plastic cylindrical bottle about 4 inches (10 cm) long and 1¼ inch (4 cm) in diameter. These bottles with foam rubber stoppers are sold as homes for fruit flies. (You can get them from Carolina Biological Supply, whose address is in the Appendix.)

Feeding your spider is the best part of keeping it. I feed mine every two to three weeks. Because they are cold-blooded, spiders need very little to eat. Warm-blooded animals use most of the energy from their food to keep their bodies warm. Web-building spiders in particular don't need much food because they spend so much time sitting still.

The growth rate of spiders and other cold-blooded animals depends in part on how much they eat. You can feed your spider every day if you like, and it will be an adult in a few short weeks. If you feed it every two or three weeks, it will stay small for months.

When the weather is warm I feed aphids to the spiders. Aphids are tiny insects that gather on the *underside* of tomato leaves, lettuce leaves, and the leaves of other garden plants. They are found on the tender new growth of some wild plants, too, such as goldenrod or thistle. (You can read more about aphids in my earlier book, *Pet Bugs,* John Wiley & Sons, 1994.)

An aphid can be about the size of the head of a straight pin, or even as small as the period at the end of this sentence. They are pear-shaped and soft-bodied, with legs so thin they are barely visible. You can collect aphids by sweeping them into a bowl with a very small paintbrush. Use the paintbrush to transfer two or three aphids to the spiderling's jar.

These little spiders also like fruit flies. (See the chapter on mantis flies for a description of how to catch fruit flies. Or you can order wingless fruit flies, which are easier to manage, from Carolina Biological Supply, whose address is in the Appendix).

What They Act Like

Spiders are predators, which means they capture other animals alive and eat them. Spiders are among the few animals that make traps to capture their prey. The trap, of course, is a web. An insect called an ant lion is an example of another animal that makes a trap to catch prey. (Ant lions are described in my earlier book, *Pet Bugs,* John Wiley & Sons, 1994.)

When I toss an aphid into one of my house spider bottles, the aphid usually gets stuck in the tangled web. Sometimes I have to gently turn the bottle over to get the aphid to fall into the web. Once the aphid is entangled, the spider will eventually sense its movements. Aphids don't move a lot, so it may take a while. Some aphids never seem to move, so I wind up putting in another aphid. When the spider does sense that something is in its web, it begins to move its front legs around, eagerly feeling the threads. The spider seems to be trying to figure out which direction the struggles are coming from. Then it dashes across the threads to the victim. But the spider doesn't bite the prey right away. Instead it begins to do a funny dance, using only its back two legs. The spider swings one rear leg forward, then the rear leg on the other side, then the one on the original side, and so on. Its whole body rocks with the alternate leg motion.

What is the spider doing? It's pulling threads from the silk glands, or spinnerets, on the tip end of its abdomen. Each rear leg reaches back to hook a thread, then swings forward to pull the thread out and wrap it around the aphid. Only the spiders in this particular family, the cobweb weavers, have tiny combs on the ends of their rear legs to guide the silk. The family is also called the "comb-footed spiders."

Within a minute or two, the prey is wrapped tightly so that it can't move. Then the spider may move it to another spot in the web, or may bite it and begin to feed. House spiders, and most other spiders, inject substances into the prey that paralyze it. They also inject digestive enzymes that turn the inside of the prey to mush. Then they suck out the insides, leaving just an empty shell. An aphid that starts out red will be white when the spider is finished—an empty exoskeleton. A house spider can take several hours to suck a fly or aphid dry. Afterward, it bites the threads around the empty husk until the remains of the meal fall from the web.

Just about every time I watch a spider eat, I see some variation I haven't seen before. It's fun to try to figure out new behaviors. If you capture and feed a spider of your own, what discoveries will you make?

How to find American House Spiderlings

SLUGS AND SNAILS _____

What They Look Like

Slugs and snails are not insects. They don't have six legs or any legs at all. They also don't have the exoskeleton that insects have. (An exoskeleton is a tough outer covering over the body.) Snails and slugs are in a phylum of animals called Mollusca, or the mollusks. This group also includes clams, squids, and octopuses, among other things. All of these animals are soft-bodied and some have shells. All have some sort of a "foot." In clams the foot is the wedge-shaped body part used to burrow into sand or mud. In octopuses and squids, the foot has developed into tentacles which can grab prey or help the animal move around. The foot of a slug or snail is the part of the body that touches the ground, as the animal creeps along from place to place.

There are hundreds of species of slugs and snails. All have a wet look to the skin, and most are smooth. Many species are brown or gray because these are good camouflage colors. But slugs do come in a variety of colors: white, yellow, and purple. Some have patterns, such as the common Leopard Slug, which is gray with black spots. A snail has a coiled shell on its back and a slug does not.

Most of the familiar slugs and land snails have two pairs of tentacles that look like little horns sticking up from the tops of their heads. The longer pair of tentacles are eyes, although they do not see very well. If you look closely, you can see a little black speck at the tip of each long tentacle. That is an eye. If you touch one, the tentacle will draw back temporarily. The shorter pair of tentacles work as noses. They detect odors or chemicals in the air.

Phylum:
Mollusca (mollusks)
Class:
Gastropoda (snails and slugs)
Order:
Stylommatophora (snails and slugs with a lung and two pairs of tentacles)
Family:
Many families and over 14,000 species
Characteristics:
Soft, fleshy body. Travel on a muscular "foot." Snails have external shells, slugs do not.
Distribution:
Throughout the United States
Food:
They are plant eaters or scavengers.

Slug

81

Where to Find Them

Slugs and snails like cool damp places. Look under logs or boards on damp ground in wooded areas. Slugs may come out in the open at night after a rain or when the dew is heavy.

In a garden you may find small slugs and snails between the wet leaves of a lettuce plant or eating vegetables. You may also find them on a damp mossy wall or between damp stones. Snails often climb trees but most slugs do not.

How to Catch Them

Take a jar with you into a wooded area. Flip over logs or any objects next to the ground. Handle slugs and snails gently. A snail's shell is delicate and will crack easily with pressure. Slugs feel sticky but they won't hurt you. Return any objects you flipped over to their original position when you're through looking.

Gently place your creature into the jar. If it will be in the jar for more than a few minutes, place in the jar in advance a damp clean sponge or damp cloth, or slightly crumpled (not wadded) damp paper towel. Put a cloth lid over the jar, secured with a rubber band.

Don't let the sun shine directly on the jar, or it will heat up rapidly and bake your animals.

How to Keep Them

If you have just a few very small slugs or snails, you can keep them right in the jar on a *slightly* crumpled, damp paper towel for a few days. The paper towel should have lots of damp nooks and crannies for your creatures to explore.

If you have a plant mister, spray the paper towel gently twice a day to keep it damp, not soggy. Or dribble a few drops of water on it with your fingers.

Keep the jar covered with a piece of cloth held in place with a rubber band. You might want to place the lid of the jar loosely over the cloth. This will keep more moisture inside the jar than the cloth alone, but will still allow some airflow.

If you want to make a more long-lasting home than a

Slug eating lettuce leaf

jar, use a small glass or plastic terrarium. Put on the bottom 1 to 2 inches (3 to 5 cm) of sand or soil. Place upon the sand or soil some leaf litter (decaying and broken leaves) from a forest floor. Add a section of rotting log, and a flattish stone. You might also put in some pieces of bark or an area of moss. Keep the piece of log, the leaves, and the rock damp by spraying the whole thing at least once a day. The soil or sand layer should stay damp, but not sodden, at all times.

Give your snails and slugs a small slice of strawberry, tomato, banana, or a very young lettuce leaf to eat. Clean the food before you give it to them so they don't eat any pesticide. Food will get moldy quickly in such a damp place, so remove uneaten food every other day or so.

Snails need calcium. To provide this, you can put a piece of cuttlebone from a pet store into the terrarium.

What They Act Like

How do slugs move if they have only one foot? They don't hop, obviously. But how else can you move on one foot?

If you put a slug or a snail on a piece of clear glass or plastic and look at it from underneath, you may be able to see how it moves. Most snails and slugs move along by waves of muscular contraction that sweep from back to front. There may be as many as eight muscular waves in motion at one time. A muscular wave looks like a long thin hump that moves from the back of the foot forward.

In some species of snails and slugs, the wave of motion reaches across the whole width of the foot. But in others the wave involves only half the width of the foot. The other side has different waves that move independently! This allows the snail to have a little more control over its direction. It also makes the snail almost seem to be walking, or maybe shuffling. Some very small snails don't move by muscular contractions, but rather by cilia. Cilia are small hairlike things that move. The movement of cilia on the foot of a small snail can move the snail along.

Helix, a garden snail

The bottom of a snail's or slug's foot has glands on it that secrete slime. Slime protects the foot from rough objects, even something as sharp as broken glass. It also leaves a trail that the snail or slug can follow the next day to return to a good food source, such as your garden lettuce, strawberry patch, or compost pile.

It doesn't matter whether you call your slug friend "he" or "she." Whichever you say will always be right. That's because each snail and slug is both a he and a she. The commonly known land snails and slugs are **hermaphrodites**—each individual has the reproductive parts of both a male and a female. This is a useful trait for animals that live alone and may not meet up with other animals of the same species very often. Any snail can mate with any other snail that it meets, of the same species. It doesn't have to wait for one of the opposite sex.

Slugs and snails have no jaws so they can't chew. They have instead a mouthpart called a radula that works like a steel file. It has lots of tiny teeth on it. The snail or slug scrapes the radula over the plant to be eaten. It shreds part of the food. Then the shredded part is swallowed.

You may notice that slugs have a big open hole on one side of their bodies. That's the opening to their "lung"—a breathing hole. Originally all mollusks lived in water and had gills. But those that now live on land had to develop a breathing chamber. It's not a true lung like ours, with little air sacs, but just a hole in the body with a lot of little blood vessels in its surface to pick up oxygen.

EARTHWORMS

What They Look Like

You have probably seen an earthworm before, and you have probably held one. Earthworms are so common, they live just about everywhere that plants grow in soil outdoors.

But there are dozens of other kinds of worms. How is the earthworm different from them? Earthworms are in a group of worms called the annelids, which means "segmented worms." If you look closely at an earthworm, you can see along its body a series of rings. It looks like its body was made of a bunch of doughnuts stacked on a broom handle. Most other segmented worms live on the ocean floor. Many of the segmented worms that live in the ocean have legs, like the genus *Nereis*. *Nereis* even has a head and eyes. It's very different from our little soil creature.

Earthworms' color ranges from pink to brown. Their size varies, too, because there are many different species of earthworms. In the eastern states we have a very long and plump earthworm that we call the night crawler. This one may stretch out as long as 10 inches (25 cm). When its body is drawn up, it may be as thick

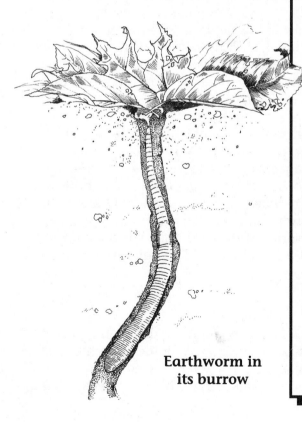

Earthworm in its burrow

Phylum:
Annelida (segmented worms)
Class:
Oligochaeta (legless segmented worms, bodies built for burrowing)
Order:
Haplotaxida (differs from other two orders in details of male reproductive structures)
Family:
Lumbricidae (common earthworms)
Characteristics:
Long, soft, obviously segmented bodies. Live in burrows in soil.
Distribution:
Throughout the United States
Food:
Decaying leaves

as ½ inch (1 cm). But most earthworms are much smaller than that. A typical garden earthworm is 3 or 4 inches (7 to 10 cm) long.

Earthworms are adapted to a burrowing lifestyle. Over evolutionary time (thousands or millions of years), they have gotten rid of body parts such as legs and eyes that are of no use to a worm living in a narrow tube or tunnel. The earthworm has tiny bristles on its body, called setae, that dig into the walls of the burrow so that the worm cannot be pulled out. It will break in half if you pull too hard.

You may have noticed that an earthworm has a brownish band around its body near the middle, like a belt or collar. It's called the clitellum and it plays a part in egg laying, which I'll describe later. You can tell which end of the worm is the mouth by looking at the clitellum. It's closer to the mouth end than to the hind end. The mouth and anus (where waste comes out) are at opposite ends of the body. On some species of earthworms, the last half or third of the body toward the hind end is flatter and wider. That's another way to tell which end is which. But this isn't true for all earthworms.

Where to Find Them

Earthworms can be found in almost any kind of soil, but they prefer loose, dark, moist soil that has a lot of rotting leaves mixed in. The type of soil in a garden is perfect, if the gardener has made an effort to improve the soil by adding rotting plant material, such as leaves or composted vegetable scraps. Also try looking under any logs or boards lying on the ground. After a rainstorm, worms can often be found on sidewalks and driveways, although many of these will be dead.

If you have trouble finding worms, you can make an area that worms will like. Pour a pan full of water over an area of bare ground (not lawn) as big as a garbage bag. Scatter a few crumbled dead leaves over the wet ground. Then put a black garbage bag over the wet area. Put a pile of leaves or grass clippings on top of the garbage bag, to weigh it down. Now wait two or three weeks. You don't need to rewet the ground unless you have no rain at all. If you do rewet it, just wet the area around the bag, not under it. If you have earthworms in the area, then you should find some under the bag when you lift it. They should be right on top of the ground.

How to Catch Them

If you find an earthworm under a log, all you have to do is gently pick it up and place it in your collecting jar. Looking in a garden or other area with loose soil is a bit tricky. If you dig into the soil with a garden spade or trowel, you're quite likely to chop worms in half. It's safer to use your hands like a steam shovel or backhoe, lifting scoops and gently looking through them. If the soil is hard, use a shovel to lift out a big chunk of soil, then gently break it apart with your hands.

If you pull at a worm that is halfway out of its burrow, you are likely to break it in two. Instead, let it go, and come up under it with your hand or a scoop of some kind.

How to Keep Them

Any terrarium or waterproof plastic container will do for keeping worms. Or if you keep them outside, a wooden box will do. I like to use a clear container, so I can see the soil all the way down. This helps me keep track of how moist the soil is. The soil should be slightly damp, but not soggy. When the soil seems to be getting dry, add water 1 tablespoon (15 ml) at a time until it's damp again. If you have only one or two very large worms or up to 10 small worms, then a glass or plastic quart jar will be big enough.

Get some loose, very dark brown soil, preferably from a healthy garden or a wooded area. Find some dead leaves (not oak) and crumble them a little by rubbing them between your hands. Sprinkle them over the top of the soil. If the soil already has bits of dead plants in it, that's good. Now add your worms to the top of the jar. Don't cover them with dirt; they'll do better digging under for themselves. At night, earthworms come out of their burrows long enough to grab the nearest food and pull it back into the burrow. In nature they seldom leave the burrow. But in captivity they may try to escape at night, especially if the soil is close to the top of the container. So put a cloth lid over the jar, held in place with a rubber band.

Worms that I have kept seem to like shredded celery leaves and used coffee grounds from a drip coffeemaker or percolator. If you give them celery leaves, or any other leafy produce like lettuce, wash it first. I've read that worms like brown sugar and cornmeal and that they will eat small pieces of vegetables. I have not noticed my own worms eating these things, but you may want to try them.

What They Act Like

Earthworms and their relatives have one talent that's very unusual in the animal kingdom. They are able to shorten and lengthen their bodies while still remaining in a straight line. Earthworms have muscles on all sides that run the entire length of the body. When those muscles contract, the body shortens. The worms have another set of muscles that encircle the body, like a bunch of tiny rubber bands around a pencil—all under the skin, of course. When these muscles contract, they squeeze the body and make it longer but thinner.

If you look at a worm, you can see that it's using both sets of muscles—stretching out, then contracting. But it doesn't stretch out all of its body at once, only one part. It stretches out the front portion to move forward, then shortens the back portion so the back can catch up with the front half. Then it starts over.

Earthworms have another odd trait, one that they share with snails and slugs. They are hermaphrodites. Each worm has the reproductive parts of both a male and a female. Each grows up to be a mother to some of its babies and a father to others. Here's how it works. Each worm has an opening in its side that contains eggs and another opening that contains sperm. The one that contains eggs is in the clitellum area. When two worms mate, they lie side by side so that one's sperm opening is lined up with the other's egg opening, and vice versa. Then each passes sperm to the other.

After earthworms have mated, each one has to make an egg sac for its own eggs. The egg sac protects the eggs until soil conditions are just right. To make the egg sac, the clitellum secretes a **gelatinous** (jellylike) ring around the worm—a ring just the same size and shape as the clitellum. The ring at first is just a covering over the clitellum. Then the worm slips out of it. As the ring passes over the worm's body, the eggs and sperm are passed into it. The gelatinous ring pinches shut and forms a little egg case about the size and shape of a grain of rice. When it hatches, only one or two tiny worms come out.

Earthworms only come out of the ground at night. But if they have no eyes, how do they know it's night? Actually, earthworms can see a little. On the top of the body, near the mouth, are some cells that are sensitive to light. They can't see objects like we can, but they can detect light. You can prove this by shining a flashlight directly on a worm's head. (Hold the light far enough away that heat is not a problem.) Most worms will turn away from the light after a few seconds.

AQUATIC PLANARIANS

What They Look Like

A young friend and I were looking for some water snails in a small pond. I pulled a leaf out of the water and turned it over. We saw on the bottom of the leaf some small black dots. They were not part of the leaf. As we watched, a couple of the spots stretched out into tiny black streaks, each one the length of a cucumber seed. "Leeches!" yelled my little friend. But they weren't leeches. They were tiny flatworms called aquatic planarians.

These funny worms are closely related to the land planarians in the next chapter. Land planarians are also flatworms. The flatworms are a

Aquatic planarians

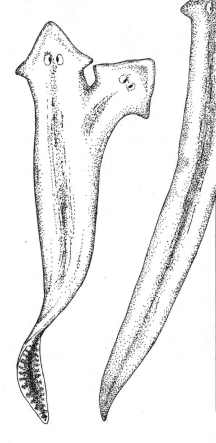

Phylum:
Platyhelminthes (flatworms)
Class:
  Turbellaria (mostly aquatic flatworms)
  Order:
    Tricladida (aquatic flatworms with three-branched digestive system and adhesive organs on the underside)
  Family:
  Planariidae
  Genus: Dugesia
  Species: Several
  Characteristics:
  Small, flat worms that cling to and creep on surfaces underwater. Often black or mottled.
Distribution:
Throughout the United States
Food:
Most are predators or scavengers of dead animal material.

large group of animals that include not only planarians but also tapeworms and flukes—two types of parasites that live in animals and sometimes in people. Planarians are not parasites, though. They live independently in nature, not inside the body of another animal.

There are many different kinds of aquatic planarians. One that is common and well-known is *Dugesia,* which has a triangular head. The points on the sides of the head are sensitive to touch and to chemicals, or smells, in the water. Not all aquatic planarians have triangular heads. Some have heads with straight sides, like tiny Popsicle sticks. Many aquatic planarians are black, but they also can be white, gray, or speckled.

Each planarian can change its length, drawing up into a tight oval when disturbed or lifted out of the water. But when an aquatic planarian is relaxed, or trying to escape, its body is like a ribbon—long, narrow, and very flat. Both the head end and the hind end of *Dugesia* can stick to a surface. This helps them change their length. It also comes in handy for moving around.

Planarians are famous for their ability to regenerate, to grow back missing parts. Many animals can grow back some missing parts. An earthworm can replace a head, a starfish an arm. A lizard can replace a tail, and a salamander can regrow an entire leg, bones and all. But planarians can do more than all of those. If a planarian's head is cut down the middle, it can grow two heads. If the head is cut repeatedly, a planarian can grow as many as 10 new heads all side by side. What's more, a planarian can be cut into several separate pieces, and have each piece grow into a whole new worm. Even a piece of the hind end, with no mouth or head, can grow into an entire body. The new worm will be smaller than the original, but will be healthy, with all its parts in working order. Planarians often pinch themselves in half on purpose in order to reproduce. Each half regrows, so there are two animals where before there was one. Some even rip themselves in half by attaching to an object and then pulling until the body tears into two pieces!

Where to Find Them

Planarians are very common in ponds, streams, and springs. I have a small homemade pond in my backyard that's the size of three bathtubs. If I pick up three or four leaves from the shallow edge of the pond, at least one is sure to have a planarian on the underside. There is one rock, about the size of a flattened basketball, that sits in the shallow water. Anytime I turn this rock over, I find dozens of planarians on the bottom.

Planarians don't swim through open water, they always seek out a surface. It may be a film on the surface of the water, but more often it is a surface underneath something.

If you are near a creek or a ditch with flowing water, you might try using bait. The moving water carries the scent of the bait. Always take an adult with you when looking in or near a body of water. Tie a thread around a small piece of raw meat, liver, or fish. A piece the size of a thumbnail or slightly larger will do. Put the meat in a shallow area of water near leaves or aquatic vegetation. Leave the other end of the thread where you can easily reach it. Pull the meat out 24 hours later. If there are planarians in the water, they'll find the meat. If your meat is gone, a fish or insect may have eaten it. Try again.

How to Catch Them

Knock the planarians off of the leaf, rock, or piece of meat into a spoon of pond water using a wet cotton swab. You can use your finger if you are very careful not to crush them.

Once you have them in the spoon, drain from the spoon any water that has meat juices in it from bait you may have used. Then put the planarians into a small container of pond water (or creek water if you caught them in a creek) for carrying them home. A quick move from warm to cool water may kill them, so make sure water temperatures are the same before transferring them. If they feel the same temperature to your finger, that's close enough.

You will need to change the water for the planarian every time you feed it, so take extra pond water home with you.

How to Keep Them

Planarians can survive a long time without eating—at least a couple of weeks, maybe much longer. The most important thing they need is pond water or springwater, preferably the water you found them in. Because they have very thin skin, planarians are probably more sensitive to water differences than aquatic insects are.

Put the pond water and your planarian into a clean bowl or cup, such as a plastic yogurt cup. I prefer a small container like this because they are easier to find and a small amount of water is easier to change. Put in a couple of fragments of dead leaves for them to hide under.

What to feed them? Many types of raw meat will do. Beef liver is a favorite. See if a parent can get a small piece of raw liver at the grocery. Wrap it in plastic wrap and freeze it. When you need a bit for your planarian, just shave off a piece the size of a watermelon seed and put the rest back in the freezer. Thaw the little piece of liver, and put it in the cup with your planarian. Leave the liver with the planarian for two or three hours or until it loses interest in the food. When the feeding is over, change the water because the beef liver juices will foul the water.

Remember when changing the water that the old and new water must be the same temperature.

How do planarians eat? The mouth is in the center of the body, on the underside. They have a tube called a **pharynx** that sticks out of the stomach for feeding. It has no teeth, but creates a sucking pressure on dead objects that causes small pieces of the food to break apart and move up the tube.

Feeding a planarian two or three times a week is plenty. It can live for weeks or even months without eating. Planarians without food will digest their own bodies and get smaller. They may eat each other.

It's important, too, to keep your cup or aquarium out of direct sunlight and away from heat vents. Warm water does not hold as much oxygen as cool water, and the planarian, like all animals and plants, needs oxygen for respiration. Water can evaporate quickly in a warm home, so check the water every day or so.

What They Act Like

Try putting your planarians in a saucer of pond water with a piece of dead leaf from the pond in the center. A saucer is a good place to watch them move for a while. Notice the different ways they move. Sometimes they move sort of like inchworms: stretching out, sticking the "adhesive organ" on the bottom of the head to the saucer, then shortening the rest of the body. But instead of making an upward loop like inchworms do, their bodies just get shorter and rounder.

At other times, instead of stretching and shortening, they appear to glide smoothly and evenly over the bottom of the saucer. When they are gliding, they are using the cilia on their skin to move. Cilia are short hair-like structures that move and can push the planarian along.

The brain of a planarian is a very simple brain, about as simple as a brain can get. But planarians are smarter than you might think. Scientists have shown in experiments that planarians can be trained and will remember their training. In one experiment, scientists Jay Best and Irvin Rubinstein put planarians (one at a time) into a Y-shaped maze. The planarian had to choose the left side of the Y or the right side. In each trial, only one side of the Y was lighted. The other side was dark. Before starting the trial, the scientists drained all the water from the maze, which made the planarian uncomfortable. The only way the worm could get the water back was to choose the lighted side of the maze. Planarians that were put in the maze many times quickly learned to choose the lighted side most of the time. A-maze-ing!

But here's an even more amazing experiment. Three scientists named James McConnell, Alan Jacobson, and Barbara Humphries trained some planarians in a different way. Then, they cut these trained planarians into pieces and fed the pieces to other planarians that had not been trained. They tested the fed planarians and found that they had learned some of the training just by eating the trained worms! Somehow the cells or chemicals that contained the memory survived being eaten and began to function in the bodies of the fed planarians.

LAND PLANARIANS

What They Look Like

If I wanted to startle someone with a creature from my yard, I would pick the land planarian. I'll never forget the first time I saw one as a child. It was traveling across a piece of slate in my backyard on a damp summer evening. The fact that it was a long, slim worm was not so odd. I'd seen lots of worms, of course. But this one was not traveling in the accordion-like manner of an earthworm. Other than its basic wormlike structure, it really looked nothing like an earthworm at all. It was 8 inches (20 cm) long and had dark stripes running the entire length of its body. It had no segments or rings around its body as an earthworm does. And it was flat, like a ribbon.

But the oddest thing of all was its head—how bizarre! The head was shaped like a half-moon or a rounded shovel. The head of this first land planarian I saw was up off the slate, like the curved bow of a ship. I had no idea what it was and didn't find out until 10 years later when I saw a picture of one in a biology textbook.

There are hundreds of species of land planarians in the tropics, but only a few in the United States. The one that's most often seen here is *Bipalmia kewense.* This species is not native to the United States, but is from the tropical forests of southeast Asia. It arrived in the United States in shipments of tropical plants. *Bipalmia kewense* was first discovered in London's Kew Gardens, a huge outdoor and indoor collection of plants from all over the world. That's why the worm is named "kewense."

When the worm is exploring, the head is very flat and thin. It flares out in front of the worm like a handheld fan. It's at least twice as wide as the body. But if you touch the head, it pulls back into the body and disappears. Along the curved outer edge of *Bipalmia*'s

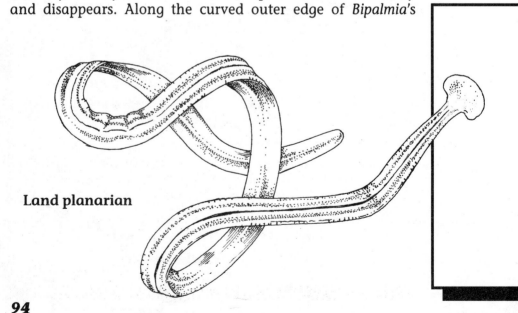

Land planarian

head are several very tiny eyes which I have not been able to see even using a six-power magnifying glass with a light on it.

The rest of its body is flattish, soft, and perfectly smooth. It glistens with slime. I've heard them described as having purple stripes on a yellowish background, but the ones I see have black or brownish stripes on a light brown or gray background.

Young ones can be as short as ½ inch (1 cm). The biggest ones I've seen have been about 8 inches (20 cm) long.

Where to Find Them

In California and the southern states, land planarians are often well established in moist yards, gardens, or woods. They also live in more northerly states, but are more likely to be found there in greenhouses protected from very cold weather.

I've found land planarians many times in the same dark, damp hideouts where I find snails, earthworms, millipedes, pill bugs, crickets, and earwigs—under logs, under rocks, under old boards on the ground. But they are not nearly as common as any of these other animals. I've never found one in the woods. They are more abundant in areas where they could have escaped from potted plants on decks or porches.

How to Catch Them

Spotting a planarian under a board is much harder than catching one. It is likely to be on the bottom of the board, coiled or bunched up into a little gray wad about as big as a thumbprint.

Phylum:	*Platyhelminthes (flatworms)*
Class:	*Turbellaria (mostly aquatic flatworms, but this one isn't)*
Order:	*Seriata (turbellarians with folded pharynx and outpocketings along the sides of the gut)*
Suborder:	*Tricladia (having a three-branched gut)*
Genus and species:	Bipalmium kewense
Characteristics:	*Long, thin, and flat. Striped from head to hind end. Shovel-shaped delicate head. Slimy and sticky.*
Distribution:	*In greenhouses throughout the United States. Escapees common, especially in warm areas.*
Food:	*Predatory on small organisms*

They are harmless, so you can easily pick one up. But be careful not to damage the planarian. Because its skin is moist and thin, any soap or salt on your skin may be absorbed into the planarian's body. Also, because the planarians are sticky and stick to your fingers, you can pull one in half without meaning to.

Place it on a damp or wet leaf or a damp bit of moss in a jar to carry it home. Cover the jar with a cloth held in place with a rubber band.

How to Keep Them

You can keep them in any size terrarium, from 6 inches (15 cm) long to 10 gallons (38 liters). But in a smaller terrarium it's easier for them to find their food, easier for you to keep the terrarium damp, and easier to keep a cloth clamped over the top. Without the cloth, they could easily crawl through any openings in the lid. If the terrarium has a snap-on lid, you can snap it on over a thin type of cloth like a handkerchief. Or you can secure the cloth with a rubber band.

Put about 2 inches (5 cm) of soil in the bottom of the terrarium. Over the soil put damp, rotting leaf litter from a forest floor. You can put a piece of damp bark in, too, for the worm to crawl under. But it's not necessary. In any case, you won't see much of the worm without turning things over.

Never put the terrarium in direct sunlight.

You might guess that these guys just eat dead leaves like earthworms do. Well, no. These worms are predators! But they have no fangs, no claws, no jaws, no speed—how could they catch any kind of prey?

Their weapon is slime. They catch very small, slow-moving prey such as tiny snails or tiny earthworms. The planarians move over the small animals and trap them in slime. The slime is so sticky that the animals can't get away. Then, as the animal struggles, the planarian eats it. The mouth is in the center of the planarian's body, on the underside. The planarian has no teeth. Like the aquatic planarian, the land planarian has a muscular tube called a pharynx that protrudes from the mouth when food is present. It may swallow the prey whole or use a sucking or pumping action to ingest the prey. Land planarians eat only at night, so you probably won't get to watch.

To feed them, look under a log or through damp leaf litter for any very small soft creatures: a tiny worm, a termite, a tiny slug or snail, or a tiny wormlike insect larva. Scatter a few of these creatures over the soil in your terrarium for your planarian to find. Or you can just put in a couple of handfuls of damp leaf litter. Make sure it is litter that has been damp for a while and right next to the ground in a shady wooded area. If you root around under the top layer of leaves on a damp forest floor, you'll find at the bottom a layer where the leaves are mashed together and rotting.

If you want to find your planarian, you may need to take out and search each leaf one at a time, putting the searched ones on a piece of newspaper until you finish. The planarian may be burrowed into the soil. You may have to dump out the whole terrarium. So you can see why it's good to have a small terrarium.

What They Act Like

Slime is a very important tool for the land planarian. In addition to helping the planarian catch its prey, slime also helps the little worm to move over sharp objects without being poked or stabbed. And it keeps the planarian from drying out as quickly as it would without slime. A land planarian can even hang upside down on a thread of slime.

Why do planarians have such oddly shaped heads? Like their close relatives the aquatic planarians, which live in water, land planarians have sensory cells and eyes on the head to feel, smell, and taste their environment, and to see light.

Anytime you have a land planarian on a damp paper towel in a room with lights on, it will sooner or later find the edge of the towel and put its head under the towel. Flip the towel over and the planarian will again find the edge and tuck its head under, away from the light. Clearly land planarians don't like light. They are nocturnal (active only at night), which helps them avoid predators. They are less likely to be seen and eaten in the dark.

Planarians, like earthworms, slugs, and snails, are hermaphrodites, which means that each is both a male and a female. When they mate, each one fertilizes the eggs of the other, so two sets of eggs are produced.

But our common species *Bipalmia kewense* does not usually reproduce sexually in the United States. (This means that it doesn't mate and lay eggs.) Since it is a native of tropical forests in southeast Asia, conditions are not quite right for sexual reproduction in the United States. So how do they reproduce? They do it by **fragmentation.** This means that they break off pieces of themselves that grow into new individuals. The new individuals are exact replicas of the original planarian, like clones.

It's quite possible that all of the land planarians in my yard, or in your yard, are clones of one another, of different ages. At any rate, I find them all uniformly charming.

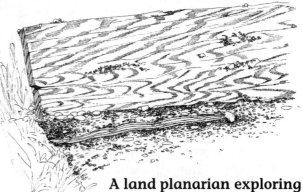

A land planarian exploring under an overturned board

CRAYFISH

What They Look Like

Crayfish are not insects, they are crustaceans. Crabs, lobsters, and pill bugs are some other familiar crustaceans. Crustaceans are similar to insects in a lot of ways. They are in the same phylum, Arthropoda. Spiders, millipedes, centipedes, and some other things are also in this phylum. Arthropoda in Latin means "jointed legs." You can see that crayfish, crabs, insects, and spiders all have legs with joints. Arthropods also have a tough outer skin that supports the body, rather than an internal skeleton like our own.

Crustaceans, insects, and spiders differ from one another in several ways. One way is in the number of legs—insects have six, spiders have eight, and in crustaceans the number varies.

Crayfish look very much like small lobsters. They range in length from ½ to 6 inches (1 to 15 cm). Most are about 4 inches (10 cm). They come in a variety of colors—blackish, brown, red, orange, green, and sometimes blue. Brown is a common color.

The body of a crayfish is shaped like a cylinder and can be divided roughly into a cephalothorax (head and thorax fused together) and an abdomen. The cephalothorax is covered with a stiff shell, or **carapace**. The abdomen has six distinct segments with joints in between that allow the abdomen to curl under. The eyes of crayfish are large and on movable stalks, like the eyes of crabs, their crustacean relatives.

Crayfish have 19 pairs of appendages! We usually think of an appendage as either an arm or a leg. And in the ancestors of the crayfish, the appendages *were* legs. But in crayfish, most of the appendages have changed over evolutionary time into structures that are very different from legs.

The first two pairs of appendages have become four antennae. The first pair of antennae are short and branched; the second pair are

Adult crayfish

very long. The next five pairs of appendages are all mouthparts, used mainly for handling food and cutting it into tiny pieces.

After the mouth, the next pair of appendages are big pincers. The crayfish picks up food with the pincers, crushes it, and tears it into pieces. The pincers are also used as weapons, in self-defense, or in attacking another animal.

Just behind the pincers are four pairs of walking legs. The first two pairs have tiny pincers of their own. The crayfish uses these walking legs when moving around and climbing. After the walking legs there are still more appendages. Each of the first five segments of the abdomen has a pair of "swimmerets," which are very thin and flimsy. You can tell a crayfish is male by looking at the first pair of swimmerets. On a female the first pair are the same as all the others. But on a male the first pair of swimmerets are much thicker, heavier, and stiffer than the others.

The last segment on the abdomen has three flat appendages, arranged to make a fan-shaped tail.

Where to Find Them

Crayfish live in freshwater, usually shallow water. Look in ponds, streams, and ditches. Always take an adult with you when looking in or near a body of water. Crayfish hide under stones and dead leaves during the day. To find one, gently lift one side of a large stone (8 to 12 inches or 20 to 30 cm across) and let it rest on its edge for a moment. Lifting the stone often creates a cloud of mud that blocks your view. As the mud settles or is swept away by the current, be very still. If the crayfish sees you, it will dart away before the water clears.

After you have looked, return the stone to its original position. Something lives under that stone, even if a crayfish doesn't. If a crayfish

Phylum:	*Arthropoda (joint-legged animals)*
Class:	*Crustacea (crustaceans)*
Order:	*Decapoda (shrimps, lobsters, crayfish, and crabs)*
Family:	*Astacidae (crayfish)*
Characteristics:	*Large, stalked, movable eyes. A shell or carapace over the cephalothorax. Segmented abdomen. Long antennae. Two large pincers.*
Distribution:	*Throughout the United States except for the Rocky Mountain area*
Food:	*Plants and dead material, sometimes live prey*

or salamander is under the rock, move the animal before you replace the rock or you may crush the animal. It will find its way back under the rock.

When looking in a ditch, gently lift any dead leaves or other plant debris that might shelter a crayfish.

Near ponds or streams you may sometimes see mounds of fresh mud up to 6 inches (15 cm) high with a hole in the center of the mound. This is a crayfish "chimney." The crayfish that build these chimneys live in underground burrows that are filled with water. Some species live only in burrows with chimneys. Some species never live in burrows, and some species live sometimes in burrows and sometimes in ponds or streams.

The burrow has one to three tunnels that come to the surface. The chimney itself is made of the mud that was taken from underground to make the burrow and tunnel. Burrow-dwelling crayfish come out at night to look for food. It would be very difficult if not impossible to dig a crayfish out of a burrow. But seeing chimneys along a stream or pond's edge is a good sign that there may be crayfish in the stream or pond.

How to Catch Them

To catch a crayfish, lay your jar behind it. Then nudge or spook the crayfish from in front. It will move backward when alarmed, into the jar. It doesn't just walk backward, it *shoots* backward. The strong, heavy muscles in its abdomen bring the fan-shaped tail down and under with lightning speed.

If the crayfish is a small one, you may be able to nudge it backward into your open palm. Be careful not to break off antennae or legs when holding it. A big crayfish might try to pinch you, so lift it by placing a finger and a thumb on either side of its body, just behind the pincers.

Transport your crayfish home in water from the pond where you caught it. Be sure not to leave the jar in a hot car or in direct sunlight. Don't leave the lid on it for more than a few minutes. The water gets fresh oxygen from fresh air above it. As soon as you get the crayfish home, put it in a container that has shallow water with a large surface area (at least 12 by 7 inches or 28 × 18 cm). If you have a very small crayfish (less than 1½ inches or 4 cm), you can put it in a baking dish with water. The water level should be at least 1 inch (3 cm) below the rim, so the crayfish can't crawl out. A baking dish is an ideal container for a small crayfish because the low sides allow lots of air movement across the water. Shallow water is essential because only the water close to the surface picks up a lot of oxygen from the air. If you have a bigger crayfish, you'll need a container with taller sides, such as an aquarium, to keep the crayfish from escaping. But still keep the water shallow. In a deep aquarium or in any jar, the water on the bottom will not have much oxygen.

A crayfish from a fast-moving stream needs even more oxygen. It will probably need an aquarium where the water is artificially aerated (has air added with an electric pump, like those used in fish tanks). Water in fast streams has more oxygen than pond water, because it picks up air bubbles as it splashes over rocks and sticks. So crayfish from these streams are adapted to oxygen-rich water.

How to Keep Them

Use pond water in your aquarium if possible, from the same place you caught the crayfish. If this is not possible, you can use bottled springwater from the grocery. Don't use distilled water.

Two inches (25 cm) of water is plenty in an aquarium with no aerator. Put in a clean stone with a sloping side so the crayfish can crawl into shallower water if it needs more air. Also put a couple of large leaves from the pond or stream into the aquarium for the crayfish to hide under.

Crayfish are mainly scavengers on plant material. But they will eat meat of almost any kind when it is available. They can even catch small fish and other live animals with their pincers. Because they are cold-blooded, they don't need to eat very often.

Try feeding your crayfish a small piece of cooked chicken or turkey, about half the size of a green pea. You can feed it every day, but twice a week is enough. Watch your crayfish eat. If it's hungry and likes the food, it will pick up a morsel with its pincers and eat right away. If the crayfish doesn't take the meat or puts it down, take the food out of the container. Any uneaten food can foul the water. Don't put any greasy food into the water, or anything that will fall apart when wet. If you see bubbles on the surface of the water, or a surface film, or the water smells bad, change it immediately. Make sure the new water is the same temperature as the old water. If it feels the same to your finger, that's close enough.

What They Act Like

Crayfish are typical crustaceans in many ways. But in one way they are unusual. Mother crayfish take care of their eggs and young babies. Most insects and crustaceans abandon their eggs as soon as they are laid. Crayfish mothers protect their eggs by attaching the eggs to their swimmerets, the small flimsy appendages along the underside of the abdomen. The mother may curl her abdomen under, too, to help the eggs stay in place. After the eggs hatch, the young crayfish cling to the swimmerets and are carried around while they are small. After they have grown and shed their skins twice, they begin to leave Mom from time to time until they leave permanently. If you catch an adult female between March and June, she may have eggs or young attached to her swimmerets.

Watching a crayfish in an aquarium, you'll notice that it spends most of its time sitting still. If it moves, it walks slowly forward on its walking legs, picking up tiny things occasionally to put in its mouth. It uses the tail muscles to scoot backward only when threatened.

You may notice that your crayfish prefers some areas of the aquarium to others. You can move things around in the aquarium to make one end of it very different from the other end. For example, you can put several small stones or leaves in one end of the aquarium, but leave the other end bare. Or try making one end darker than the other by putting a dark cover over it. You could also prop up one end of the aquarium by putting a book under it, so that the water is deeper at one end. Then check the crayfish's location every five minutes for an hour to see which end it likes best.

**Crayfish burrow
and "chimneys"**

APPENDIX
Animal Classification

Animals are grouped into categories based on their similarity to one another and on their evolutionary relationships. The primary, or largest, divisions of the animal kingdom are **phyla**. There are about 26 phyla of animals, depending on whose system of classification you use. Humans are in the phylum Chordata. This phylum includes all animals with backbones (fish, amphibians, reptiles, birds, and mammals) and a few other small obscure animals.

Insects are in the phylum Arthropoda. Some other members of this phylum, called arthropods, are the spiders, the crustaceans, the millipedes, and the centipedes. Most of the animals in this book are in the phylum Arthropoda. This phylum, and all phyla, are divided into **classes.** The three classes of arthropods described in the book are Insecta (insects), Arachnida (spiders and their kin), and Crustacea (crustaceans).

Another phylum represented in this book is the phylum Mollusca. The mollusks are divided into three classes: the Cephalopoda (squids and octopuses), the Bivalvia (clams and similar animals), and the Gastropoda (snails and slugs). Only the snails and slugs are in this book.

One more phylum found in the book is that of the segmented worms, Annelida. The earthworms in this book are a type of segmented worm.

And lastly, the flatworms appear here, too, of the phylum Platyhelminthes. Most types of flatworms are parasitic, but the free-living flatworms in this book are not. Included in the book are both aquatic flatworms and land flatworms. Both are commonly called planarians.

Each class is divided into **orders.** The arthropods in this book represent nine orders within the class Insecta, one order in the class Arachnida, and one order in the class Crustacea.

Orders are further divided into **families,** which are likewise divided into **genera** and then **species.** Animals within each division have something in common, such as wing structure. Two animals in the same genus have more features in common than two animals in the same family. Two animals in the same order have more features in common than two animals in the same class, and so on. The only animals that are capable of interbreeding, or mating, successfully in nature are those in the same species.

The system of classification is as follows, with the largest category first and the smallest category last:

Phylum
   Class
      Order
         Family
            Genus
               Species

Phylum Arthropoda

The phylum Arthropoda includes most of the animals in this book. It includes insects, spiders, crustaceans, millipedes, and many more. Arthropoda means "jointed foot." Arthropods do not have backbones; they have jointed legs and most have an exoskeleton, or hard outer covering made of a tough substance called chitin. This exoskeleton is shed or molted periodically. All have a brain, and a nerve cord that runs along the underside of the body instead of down the back.

Class Insecta

Insects are one group of arthropods. Insects' bodies are divided into three regions: the head, a middle section called the thorax, and a rear section called the abdomen. Attached to the thorax are three pairs of jointed legs. Most insects, but not all, have two pairs of wings attached to the thorax. Some have one pair of wings, and some have none. Insects have one pair of antennae.

Order Coleoptera   The insect order Coleoptera includes only the beetles. It is the largest order of insects, with over 300,000 species. They have hard bodies and chewing mouthparts. Adults have two pairs of wings. The outer pair are really wing covers, called elytra. These meet in a straight line down the middle of the beetle's back, and form a hard cover over the back when the beetle is not flying. The name Coleoptera means "sheath wings," a reference to these elytra. The inner pair of wings, used for flying, are thin and clear, and not visible at rest. In flight, the elytra are flipped up and forward, out of the way.

Beetle larvae are wormlike and segmented. They are often soft-bodied and whitish, with a distinct head and six legs just behind the head. Many beetle larvae are called **grubs.** After growing, the larvae turn into pupae and undergo complete metamorphosis. The diet varies.

Order Dermaptera   The order Dermaptera includes only the earwigs. *Derm* means "skin" and *aptera* means "without wings." A few species of earwigs are wingless, and the others have very short wings, so that the top of the abdomen is exposed. This exposed "skin" must be the source of the name.

Earwigs have one large pair of pincers on the hind end that make them easily recognizable. Most are plant eaters or scavengers. A **scavenger** is an animal that eats dead plant or animal matter. They are usually found under logs or other objects on the ground, or on plants. They may be found in homes.

Earwigs undergo gradual metamorphosis, so the young are not larvae but are nymphs. Many female earwigs guard the nymphs when they are small.

Order Hemiptera   Hemiptera is the order of true bugs. Insects that are not hemipterans are often called bugs. But to a scientist, "bug" means an insect in the order Hemiptera, just as "beetle" means an insect in the order Coleoptera.

All hemipterans have a long, tubelike, sucking mouthpart. Those that are predators stick the tube into their prey and suck out body fluids. Those that are plant eaters use the tube to pierce plants and suck out plant juices.

A hemipteran can be identified as such by the pattern on its back, created by the wings. *Hemi* means "half" and *ptera* means "wing." Each wing is half thick and leathery and half thin and clear. These odd wings overlap one another when closed. The half-and-half aspect of the overlapped wings creates an X on the back. It is present on all hemipterans, but more obvious on some than others.

Hemipterans undergo gradual metamorphosis. The young are nymphs that feed in the same manner as their parents, and gradually grow up without any pupal stage.

Order Hymenoptera   These are the ants, wasps, bees, and a few others. Most species in the order Hymenoptera are solitary and do not live in colonies. But the most well-known members of the order are those that live in complex social groups. The colonies of these so-called **social insects** typically have a **queen** that lays eggs, and female **workers** that don't reproduce but take care of the queen and her young.

Some hymenopterans are wingless as adults, others have two pairs of clear wings. All adults have chewing mouthparts. Bees, ants, and wasps have a pinched-in middle, or waist. The sawflies and their kin do not.

Hymenopterans undergo complete metamorphosis, having a larval and a pupal stage. Many construct a nest for their eggs.

Many hymenopterans are important pollinators of plants, especially the bees. A **pollinator** is an animal that carries pollen from one flower to the next as it travels. This is an important service, because flowers must have pollen from another flower in order to make seeds and fruits.

Order Lepidoptera   The order Lepidoptera includes only the butterflies and moths. The name Lepidoptera means "scale wings," an appropriate name because the wings, body, and legs are covered with colored scales. The scales come off easily if the butterfly or moth gets stuck in a spiderweb, helping it escape.

A butterfly or moth has a soft body and a coiled strawlike mouthpart for sucking flower **nectar,** a sugary fluid produced by flowers to attract pollinators. The long, wormlike larvae, called **caterpillars,** have chewing mouthparts and usually eat leaves. When full-size, the caterpillars form an envelope in which to pass the pupal stage. The envelope of moths is often made of silk and called a **cocoon,** while that of butterflies, called a **chrysalis,** is made of toughened skin. Inside the cocoon or chrysalis, the insects turn into adults. Because they have this pupal stage, they are said to undergo complete metamorphosis.

Order Neuroptera   The order Neuroptera includes mantis flies, ant lions, lacewings, dobsonflies, and snakeflies. Neuroptera means "nerve wings" (*neuro* means "nerve" and *ptera* means "wings"). All have two pairs of clear wings with many visible veins. The network of veins looks like a network of nerves, which is where the name came from. Adults have chewing (as opposed to piercing and sucking) mouthparts, and some are predators. All the larvae are predators. Antennae are long. All neuropterans undergo complete metamorphosis, so the young are called larvae and look very different from the parents.

Order Odonata   This is the order of dragonflies and damselflies. All odonates have four long, clear wings. Each wing is crisscrossed by a network of veins. Dragonflies hold all four wings out straight like airplane wings when at rest. Damselflies hold the wings together over the body while resting.

The compound eyes of odonates are huge and take up most of the space on the large head. (A compound eye is an eye composed of many separate visual units.) Dragonflies can be up to $3\frac{1}{2}$ inches (9 cm) long. The long, slender abdomen takes up most of this length.

Odonates undergo gradual metamorphosis. The nymphs, sometimes called **naiads,** live in water. Both adults and nymphs are predatory.

Order Orthoptera   The insect order Orthoptera includes crickets, grasshoppers, praying mantises, and walkingsticks, among others. Orthoptera means "straight wings." All orthopterans have two pairs of wings, but only the front pair are visible when the insects are not flying. Many orthopterans "sing" by rubbing one body part against another. Crickets sing or chirp by rubbing one wing against the other.

All orthopterans have chewing mouthparts (as opposed to piercing or sucking ones), and most eat plants. All have a pair of projections on the hind end of the abdomen called **cerci.** The cerci, which are long on crickets, serve as feelers. The cerci on walkingsticks and mantises are shorter but easy to see.

Most orthopterans have long, hairlike antennae, which also serve as feelers. Some use their antennae to communicate with each other by touch.

Class Crustacea

The crustaceans are a large class of mostly aquatic joint-legged animals that have a hard exoskeleton, a pair of appendages (usually legs) on each body segment, and two pairs of antennae. This class includes shrimps, lobsters, crabs, barnacles, and many more. Crustaceans are related to insects because they're both in the phylum Arthropoda, the joint-legged animals with exoskeletons. But insects are not crustaceans and crustaceans are not insects.

Order Decapoda   The decapods are the shrimps, crayfish, lobsters, and crabs. Most decapods are marine creatures, but the crayfish and some crabs and shrimps live in freshwater. A few crabs are terrestrial. Decopods have five pairs of walking legs on the thorax. These ten walking legs give the order its name (*deca* means "ten" and *poda* means "legs"). In many decapods, including the crayfish, the first pair of walking legs are modified into pincers.

Class Arachnida

This is a class of mostly air-breathing, joint-legged animals. It includes spiders and scorpions, mites, ticks, and harvestmen. The body of arachnids is divided into two regions, the abdomen and a front region called the **cephalothorax,** which bears four pairs of legs but no antennae. In some arachnids the two body regions appear to be fused.

Order Araneae   The order Araneae contains only the spiders. It is composed of arachnids whose cephalothorax has a shieldlike covering, on which are set the simple eyes, usually eight in number. (A simple eye is composed of only one visual unit, unlike the compound eye of many insects. Simple eyes do not see as well as compound eyes.) The jaws of a spider are sharp and pointed and used for injecting prey with poison. Near the jaws are two feelerlike organs called pedipalps, used for holding prey and for feeling. The tip of the abdomen usually has three pairs of **spinnerets,** organs that contain silk glands for producing threads of silk. Each spinneret has a nozzlelike opening.

Phylum Mollusca

The phylum Mollusca includes all the animals commonly called mollusks. Snails, slugs, octopuses, squids, clams, oysters, and their kin are all mollusks. Mollusks are soft-bodied and lack any kind of internal skeleton. Many have a shell. Some of the mollusks without shells, such as squids and slugs, have a simple internal rigid structure that is not a skeleton, but is an evolutionary leftover from the shells of their ancestors.

Some mollusks have a head with a mouth, sense organs, and a very simple brain. All have a visceral mass, which corresponds to our torso and contains most of the internal organs, and a mantle. The mantle is part of the body wall and secretes the shell, if there is one. All mollusks have some sort of "foot," which is the lower muscular part of the body used for moving around.

Three of the more commonly known classes of mollusks are the Gastropoda (snails and slugs), the Bivalvia (clams, oysters, mussels, scallops, etc.), and the Cephalopoda (octopuses, squids, and their kin). The bivalves all live in water and have a foot that serves as a muscular wedge for burrowing. The cephalopods all live in water, too. The "foot" of a cephalopod has evolved into tentacles.

Class Gastropoda

This class of mollusks includes the snails and slugs. In the gastropods, the mollusk foot is a flat, creeping sole that often leaves a mucus trail behind. Most gastropods live in the sea, but the ones in this book live on land. Seasnails and sea slugs may be very brightly colored.

Order Stylommatophora   These mollusks have two pairs of tentacles, the second pair with eyes at the tip. It includes many terrestrial snails (including the common genus *Helix*) and many terrestrial slugs (including the Leopard Slug, genus *Limax*).

Phylum Annelida

The phylum Annelida consists of three classes: the Hirudinea (leeches), the Polychaeta (sea worms, many with well-developed legs), and the Oligochaeta (the earthworms and their kin).

An annelid has a long, cylindrical (tubular) body that is composed of segments. The seams between the segments look like rings. The annelids are more advanced than the flatworms. Their digestive system is more developed, in having two openings, both a mouth and an anus. Their segmentation is evidence of their close relationship to the arthropods, the most advanced of the invertebrates.

Class Oligochaeta

This class includes all of the earthworms, and many other annelids that live in freshwater. Some are burrowers, others live in underwater vegetation. Most oligochaetes have setae, very small projections from the skin that anchor the worm in its burrow.

Order Haplotaxida This order includes the common earthworm (genus *Lumbricus*), as well as many others, some of which live in water.

Phylum Platyhelminthes

The phylum Platyhelminthes includes the flatworms. Their bodies are very thin or compressed in comparison with their width and length, as though they have been run over. Flatworms are much more primitive than the arthropods or the mollusks. They have only one opening into the digestive system, which serves as both mouth and anus. They are so flat that they don't need a respiratory system. Each cell is close enough to the surface to get oxygen directly from the air. There are three classes of flatworms: the Trematoda (parasitic flukes), the Cestoidea (parasitic tapeworms), and the Turbellaria (includes the free-living planarians in this book).

Class Turbellaria

This class is mostly free-living flatworms. Most turbellarians live in the sea, many others live in freshwater. Only a few are terrestrial. The skin of turbellarians is covered with **cilia,** which are small hairlike projections that move. Turbellarians can creep across a surface by the movement of their cilia. These worms can be oval-shaped or long and narrow. Most are small, but some land planarians can reach 2 feet (60 cm) in length.

Order Seriata The order Seriata includes both the aquatic planarians and the land planarians in this book. All members of this order have outpocketings of the digestive system that increase the amount of surface area for absorption.

To order milkweed bugs, fruit flies as food for spiderlings and mantis flies, insect nets, aquatic nets, fruit fly vials or bottles for spiderlings, and more, contact:

> Carolina Biological Supply Company
> 2700 York Road
> Burlington, NC 27215
> 1.800.584.0381
>
>
> Ward's Biology
> P.O. Box 92912
> Rochester, NY 14692
> 1.800.962.2660

GLOSSARY

abdomen   The hind section of the body of an insect or other arthropod, behind the thorax.

carapace   The hard outer covering over the cephalothorax of crustaceans.

caterpillar   The long, wormlike larva of a butterfly or moth.

cephalothorax   A body region in crustaceans and arachnids consisting of the head and the thorax fused together.

cerci (singular **cercus**)   A pair of projections on the hind end of the abdo-110men of some insects and other arthropods. Some cerci are used as feelers.

chrysalis   A protective capsule enclosing a pupa as it transforms from larva to adult, often specifically used to mean the casing of tough skin around a butterfly pupa.

cilia   Tightly packed rows of short hairlike structures that grow out of the surface of some creatures and help them to move.

class   A major category of biological classification ranking above an order and below a phylum, and composed of related orders.

cocoon   An envelope, often made of silk, that a moth larva forms around itself and in which it passes the pupal stage.

cold-blooded   Having a body temperature that varies with the temperature of the surroundings.

complete metamorphosis   See **metamorphosis.**

compound eye   An eye (as of an insect) made up of many separate visual units.

echolocation   The practice of locating objects by making sounds that bounce off the objects and return to the animal.

elytra (singular **elytron**)   The thickened, hard, or leathery first pair of wings that function as wing covers in beetles and earwigs, and form the hard back of beetles at rest.

exoskeleton   The hard outer covering of an arthropod's body.

family   A category of biological classification ranking above a genus and below an order, and usually composed of several genera.

fragmentation   The process of reproducing by breaking off pieces of the body that grow into new individuals.

fras   The feces, or bodily waste, of a caterpillar.

gelatinous   Jellylike.

genus (plural **genera**)   A category of biological classification ranking above a species and below a family, and composed of related species.

gradual metamorphosis   See **metamorphosis.**

grub   The wormlike larva of many types of beetles.

hermaphrodite   An individual animal that has both male and female reproductive organs.

incomplete metamorphosis   See **metamorphosis.**

larva (plural **larvae**)   A wormlike immature insect that is very different in shape and lifestyle from the adult and that undergoes complete metamorphosis.

maxillary palps   Feelerlike structures on the mouthparts of insects, sometimes used to feel the ground for food, as in camel crickets.

membranous   Thin and more or less transparent.

metamorphosis   A change in body form during development. A gradual and small change, as occurs with all hemipterans, camel crickets, grasshoppers, and earwigs is called **gradual** or **incomplete metamorphosis.** An abrupt and great change, as occurs in the cocoon of a moth, is called **complete metamorphosis.**

migrate   To travel each year from one region or climate to another for feeding or breeding.

molt   To shed the exoskeleton after a period of growth, as in arthropods.

naiad   A nymph of a dragonfly or damselfly, so named because it lives in water (naiads were water nymphs in classical mythology).

nectar   A sugary substance produced by flowers to attract pollinators.

nocturnal   Active at night.

nymph   The young stage of any insect species that undergoes gradual metamorphosis.

order   A category of biological classification ranking above a family and below a class, and composed of related families.

ovipositor   A long, thin structure on the hind end of the body of some insects, such as camel crickets, which is used to deposit their eggs.

palps   See **maxillary palps.**

parasite   An animal that feeds, grows, and is sheltered on another animal but does not kill it, at least not right away.

pharynx   In general, the upper portion of the throat leading to the esophagus. In planarians, the pharynx projects from the body as a long tube for ingesting food.

phylum (plural **phyla**)   One of the primary divisions of the animal kingdom, ranking above a class and below a kingdom, and composed of related classes.

pollinator   An animal, usually an insect or hummingbird, that transports pollen from the male reproductive parts on one flower to the female reproductive parts on another flower. This usually happens as a result of the animal's flying from flower to flower in search of nectar.

predator   An animal that kills and eats other animals.

proboscis   A long, tubular mouthpart, as in butterflies and moths, and hemipterans.

prolegs   The hind legs of a caterpillar, used for grasping and not present in the adult.

pronotum   The top covering of the prothorax of an insect. In many insects, it is large and conspicuous and provides the top cover of the body between the head and the base of the wings

prothorax   The first of the three segments of the thorax of an insect, bearing the first pair of legs. The prothorax in mantises and mantis flies is very long.

pupa (plural **pupae**)   In insects with complete metamorphosis, the stage of development where the larva changes to the adult form. To **pupate** is to undergo this process.

queen   The fertile female member of a colony of social insects whose main function is to lay eggs. The queen is fed and tended by workers.

scavenger   An animal that eats dead plant or animal matter.

social insects   The ants, bees, termites, and wasps, all of which live in colonies with complex social lives.

soldier   A member of a colony of social insects that uses its large head and jaws to defend the colony by attacking and biting enemies. Soldiers are not able to reproduce.

species (plural **species**)   A category of biological classification ranking below a genus, and composed of animals or plants capable of interbreeding.

spinneret   An organ with a nozzlelike opening which contains silk glands for producing threads of silk. The spinnerets of caterpillars are near the mouth. Those of spiders are on the tip of the abdomen.

spiracles   Openings in an insect's body that lead into the trachea, or breathing tubules.

surface tension   The force that holds water molecules together at the surface.

swarm   A large group of moving insects.

thigmotaxic   Being attracted to spaces where the body is in contact with more than one surface, such as crevices.

thorax   The body region behind the head of an insect which bears the legs and wings.

warm-blooded   Having a body temperature that is regulated internally and stays constant.

worker   A member of a colony of social insects whose job is to feed and tend the queen and her eggs and larvae, to make repairs on the nest, and so on.

FOR FURTHER READING

Borror, Donald, and Richard White. *A Field Guide to the Insects.* Peterson Field Guide Series. Boston: Houghton Mifflin, 1970.

> If I could have only one field guide to the insects, I would keep this one.

Goor, Ron, and Nancy Goor. *Insect Metamorphosis.* New York: Macmillan, 1990.

> This book has beautiful color photographs of an assortment of insects in various stages of their life cycles.

Kneidel, Sally. *Classroom Critters and the Scientific Method.* Golden, Colo.: Fulcrum, 1999.

> This one describes experiments and science projects you can do with gerbils, mice, goldfish, guppies, hamsters, lizards, kittens, and puppies. It also explains the steps and principles of the scientific method.

Kneidel, Sally Stenhouse. *Creepy Crawlies and the Scientific Method.* Golden, Colo.: Fulcrum, 1993.

> This book describes experiments and science projects you can do with common insects, tadpoles, toads, earthworms, pillbugs, and other animals. It also explains the steps and principles of the scientific method.

Kneidel, Sally. *Pet Bugs.* New York: John Wiley & Sons, 1994.

> This has the same format as *More Pet Bugs,* but describes 26 other creatures, mostly insects.

Kneidel, Sally. *Slugs, Bugs, and Salamanders: Discovering Animals in Your Garden.* Golden, Colo.: Fulcrum, 1997.

> In this book you'll find experiments that reveal the connections among common garden plants, the pests that eat them, and predators that eat the pests. Provides a map for a garden that includes homes for helpful animals.

Laughlin, Robin Kittrell. *Backyard Bugs.* San Francisco: Chronicle Books, 1996.

> This book has wonderful color photographs with accompanying text. The text is unusual and interesting, often just an anecdote about how the insect was caught.

Lavies, Bianca. *Backyard Hunter, Praying Mantis.* New York: Dutton, 1990.
Impressive color photographs of mantises in every stage of life,
including hatching from the egg case.

Lavies, Bianca. *Compost Critters.* New York: Dutton, 1993.
Most of the book is about the animals that live in and feed on compost and how they break it down.

Leahy, Christopher. *Peterson First Guide to Insects of North America.* Boston:
Houghton Mifflin, 1987.
A much more limited insect field guide than the standard Peterson
guide by Borror and White described above. But it's easier for children
to use and fits easily into a shirt pocket.

Milne, Lorus, and Margery Milne. *The Audubon Society Field Guide to North
American Insects and Spiders.* New York: Alfred A. Knopf, 1990.
The color photographs make this book fun for browsing. Only rela-
tively common species are illustrated.

Milord, Susan. *The Kids' Nature Book.* Charlotte, Vt.: Williamson, 1989.
This book describes one nature activity for each day of the calendar
year.

Shepherd, Elizabeth. *No Bones.* New York: Macmillan, 1988.
Here you'll find descriptions of commonly found small arthropods—
animals without backbones. Some are insects.

VanCleave, Janice. *Insects and Spiders: Mind-Boggling Experiments You Can
Turn into Science Fair Projects.* New York: John Wiley & Sons, 1998.
Lots of interesting information and activities in this book.

White, Richard. *A Field Guide to the Beetles.* Peterson Field Guide series.
Boston: Houghton Mifflin, 1983.
A thorough enough coverage of beetles, with much more informa-
tion on this group than you'll find in an insect field guide.

Zim, Herbert, and Clarence Cottom. *Insects.* Racine, Wis.: Golden Press of
Racine, 1987.
This is a simpler guide than the standard Peterson guide, and more
usable for children. Its coverage, though, is limited.

INDEX